COLLEEN ANDERSON

THE STEP BY STEP ART OF
Paper Crafts

CLB 3109
This edition published 1994 by Whitecap Books Ltd.
1086 West 3rd Street, North Vancouver, B.C.,
Canada V7P 3J6
© 1994 CLB Publishing Ltd., Godalming,
Surrey, England
Printed and Bound in Singapore by Tien Wah Press
ISBN 1-55110-244-7

THE STEP BY STEP ART OF

Paper Crafts

Text and Paper Designs by
CHERYL OWEN

Photography by
NEIL SUTHERLAND & STEVE TANNER

WHITECAP BOOKS

Contents

Equipment

Much of the equipment needed for paper crafts falls within the standard desk range, which you probably already possess. For comfort and safety, work on a flat, clean surface taking care to keep sharp implements, glues and paints well out of the reach of children.

For Drawing and Painting

For paper crafts an HB pencil is best – keep sharpened to a fine point for accurate drawing, or use a propelling pencil. Always use a ruler and a set square when drawing squares and rectangles so that the angles are accurate. Draw circles with a compass or a circle stencil for miniature circles.

Many of the projects in this book are painted. Craft paints, such as poster paints, are the most versatile. The colours mix easily, dry quickly, and most are non-toxic. Watercolour paints give a soft, blended effect. For best results, use a paintbrush suitable for the type of paint you are using. Spray paints are fun to experiment with – if sprayed lightly, a shaded, subtle effect is achieved. Always spray in a well ventilated room and protect the area with newspaper. Please use sprays that are free from CFCs.

For Cutting

Sharp, pointed scissors are vital for paper crafts. Choose scissors that feel comfortable; a small pair are best for cutting detailed shapes. However, craft knives give a neater cut than scissors – always use on a cutting mat and replace the blades often, since a blunt blade will tear the paper or card.

Use wire cutters to cut wire and a small hacksaw to cut wooden dowelling.

For Sticking

Always read the manufacturer's instructions for adhesives and test them on scrap paper before use. When gluing thin papers together ensure the glue does not seep to the surface. Also, take care that the glue does not smudge the design on printed papers. A plastic spreader or strip of card is useful for distributing the glue evenly.

Spray glues give a professional finish, but they must be used in a well ventilated atmosphere with the surrounding area protected with newspaper.

PVA adhesive is a non-toxic solution that dries to a clear, glossy finish, so it can also be used as a varnish.

Double-sided adhesive tape is a clean alternative to glue. The tape is adhesive on both sides with a backing tape that can be removed when ready for application.

Masking tape is preferable to clear, adhesive tape, which dries out very quickly. It is a low-tack tape, which means that it can be used to hold paper and templates in position and later removed without marking the surface.

Materials

Card and Paper

There is a vast range of card and paper available for craft use nowadays, much of which you will already have. Cardboard packets and boxes can be cut up and covered with coloured papers. Save any left-over wallpaper, giftwrappings or paper bags printed with attractive designs.

Most of the card used in this book is thin and lightweight, like that used for cereal packets. When thick card is required, it should be sturdy enough to crease if bent. Since card does not fold easily, you will need to score along any proposed folds with a craft knife so the card folds smoothly.

Some card has a glossy or metallic coating on one side, and you can create your own card of this kind by applying a paper of your choice to matt card with spray glue.

Foam board consists of a layer of foam sandwiched between 2 layers of cardboard. It is exceptionally lightweight and is available in a variety of thicknesses.

Crepe paper is a highly versatile material and especially useful for flower-making, since it will stretch when the grain is gently pulled apart. When cutting, match any arrow on the template with the grain on the crepe paper.

Paper ribbon is similar in appearance to crepe paper. It is a strip of randomly creased paper that comes in the form of a twisted rope. Simply unravel the strip to use it flat.

Tissue paper is rather delicate but 2 layers can be spray glued together to make it stronger and more dense.

Colourful gummed papers and stickers are easy to use. To attach small non self-adhesive paper shapes, apply double-sided adhesive tape to the reverse before cutting out. Then peel away the backing paper and place in position.

Sophisticated projects often benefit from the use of unusual papers. Specialist art shops stock handmade textured and marbled papers which, although expensive, make a handcrafted model extra special.

Craft Components

Many of the materials used in paper crafts come from craft suppliers and are inexpensive to buy. Cotton pulp or polystyrene balls can be painted or covered with tissue paper. Stick-on 'joggle' eyes add a humorous touch and toy safety eyes are highly realistic. Coloured feathers and woollen pompoms offer a frivolous change of texture.

Look out for other interesting decorations. Beads and sequins can give a theatrical feel, while natural materials such as fir cones and dried flowers add a rustic touch. Small fresh fruits mixed with paper creations lend an exotic air.

Giftwrapping ribbons are also effective, with metallic, irridescent and glossy varieties among the many options available. Narrow giftwrapping ribbons curl attractively when pulled smoothly over the blade of a pair of scissors.

Wooden dowelling – a basis for some of the trees in this book – is available in different thicknesses and can be painted.

Floral Accessories

Florists, garden centres and suppliers as well as craft shops stock many accessories for floral projects. Dry foam is a grey plastic foam used as a basis for dried and artificial arrangements. It comes in various shapes and sizes – rings, cones, balls or blocks – and can be cut easily with a craft knife. Dried and artificial flowers can be glued on or inserted on wires. The foam can be concealed by covering with crepe paper or tissue paper.

Stamen strings, available from craft shops and suppliers, are short strings that have solid, coloured ends. Cut in half, they are used as stamens or flower centres.

Wire comes in many different thicknesses. Fine wire, often called stub wire, is widely used for making flowers. Garden centres offer a thick wire designed for bonsai trees. It bends easily and is useful for forming armateurs (see the orange tree on page 58). Green wire does not need covering.

Floral tape is a fine, plastic tape – usually green – that is bound around wires and flowers to join wires together.

Techniques

The same basic methods occur in many of the projects. Therefore, you will need to read the techniques described here carefully before you begin any projects. It is also advisable to practise on spare scraps of paper and card if you are new to the craft.

Paper flowers and foliage appear throughout the book. Refer to the photographs of the finished projects as well as real flowers and leaves to help you make them appear as realistic as possible. When you have mastered the techniques, you will be able to recreate other favourite flowers from the garden in paper. Alternatively, be bold and design your own fantasy flowers.

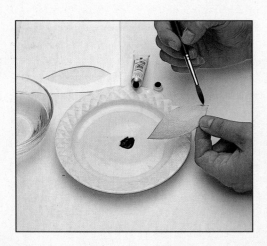

Watercolour Method

1 *Cut leaves or petals from watercolour paper. Dampen, then paint a pale shade with watercolour paint. Before the paint dries, paint a slightly darker shade at the base, blending the colour upwards.*

2 *If you wish, paint 'veins' on the leaves in a darker shade with a fine paintbrush. Finish with the 'single layer method' shown to the right.*

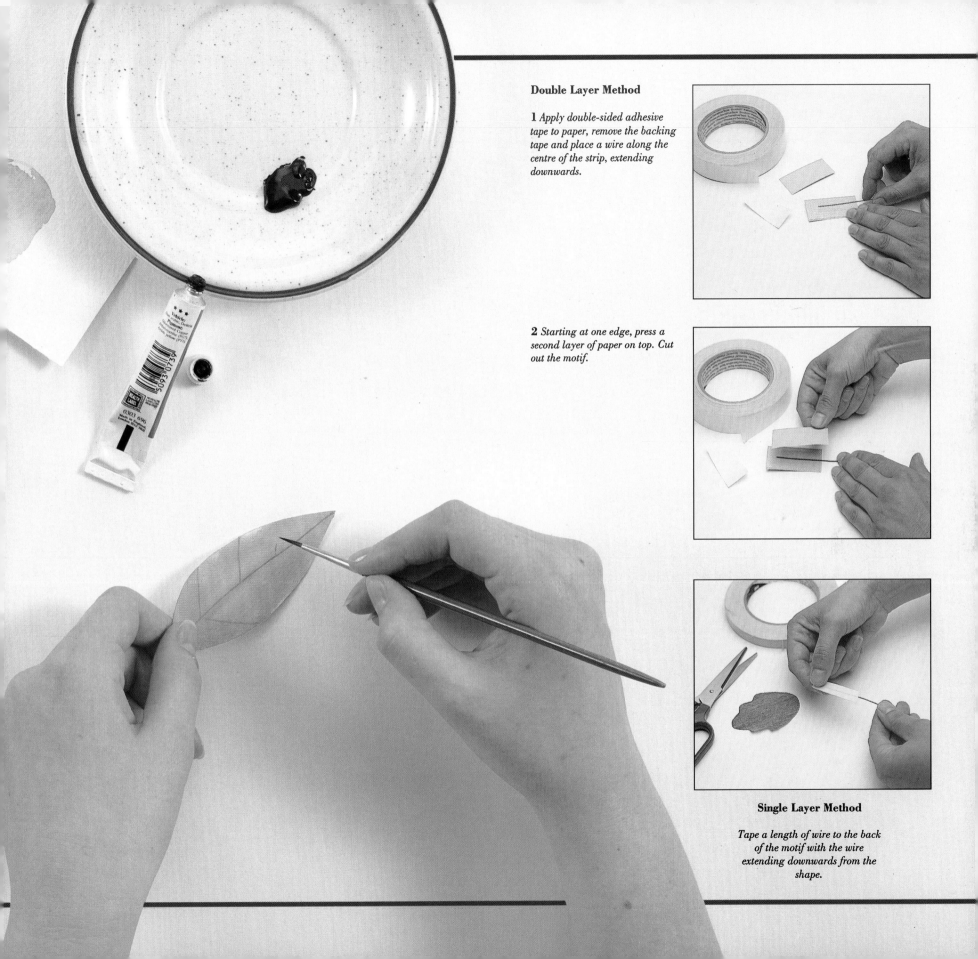

Double Layer Method

1 *Apply double-sided adhesive tape to paper, remove the backing tape and place a wire along the centre of the strip, extending downwards.*

2 *Starting at one edge, press a second layer of paper on top. Cut out the motif.*

Single Layer Method

Tape a length of wire to the back of the motif with the wire extending downwards from the shape.

Poppies, Anemone and Buttercup

1 *To make the flower centre, bend the end of a length of wire into a hook. Wrap a ball of cotton wool around the hook. Cut a 4-cm (1½-in) diameter circle of green tissue paper for the poppies, a 5-cm (2-in) diameter circle of black crepe paper for an anemone or a 2.5-cm (1-in) diameter circle of yellow crepe paper for a buttercup. Wrap the circle over the cotton wool and glue the circumference to the wire.*

Fringed Stamens

Many of the flowers have stamens formed from a fringed strip of crepe paper or tissue. Cut a strip of the paper, then cut a fringe along one long edge, ending 4 mm (³⁄₁₆ in) from the opposite edge. Cut the ends of the fringe diagonally to make points.

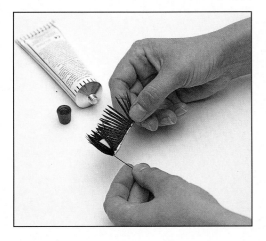

2 *Cut a strip of yellow tissue paper 7.5 x 3.5 cm (3 x 1½ in) for a Himalayan poppy or black crepe paper for a field poppy. Cut a strip of black crepe paper 25 x 3.5 cm (10 x 1½ in) for an anemone. Cut a strip of yellow tissue paper 4 x 1 cm (1½ x ⅜ in) for a buttercup. Make fringed stamens as described above. Spread glue along the lower edge and bind the stamens around the flower centre.*

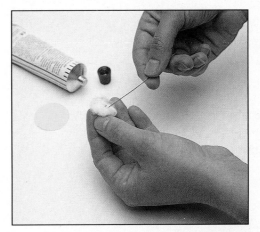

Daisies

1 *Bend the end of a length of wire into a hook. Wrap a ball of cotton wool around the hook and flatten it slightly to make the daisy centre. From yellow crepe paper, cut a 2.5-cm (1-in) diameter circle for a small daisy or a 3.5-cm (1½-in) diameter circle for a large daisy. Wrap the circle over the cotton wool and glue the circumference to the wire.*

2 *Use the templates on page 106 to cut one small daisy from white crepe paper or 2 large daisies from white paper. Make a hole in the centre. Dab glue sparingly onto the underside of the flower centre and insert the wire down through the holes. Push the daisies up against the flower centre. Bind floral tape around the stem.*

3 *Referring to templates on pages 106-107, cut 6 petals from bright blue crepe paper for a Himalayan poppy, red crepe paper for a field poppy and red, pink or mauve crepe paper for an anemone. Apply 2 layers of yellow tissue paper together for a buttercup with spray glue and cut 6 petals (template on page 106). Gently stretch the crepe paper petals widthways. Glue the petals around the flower centre. Bind floral tape around the base of the flower and wire stem.*

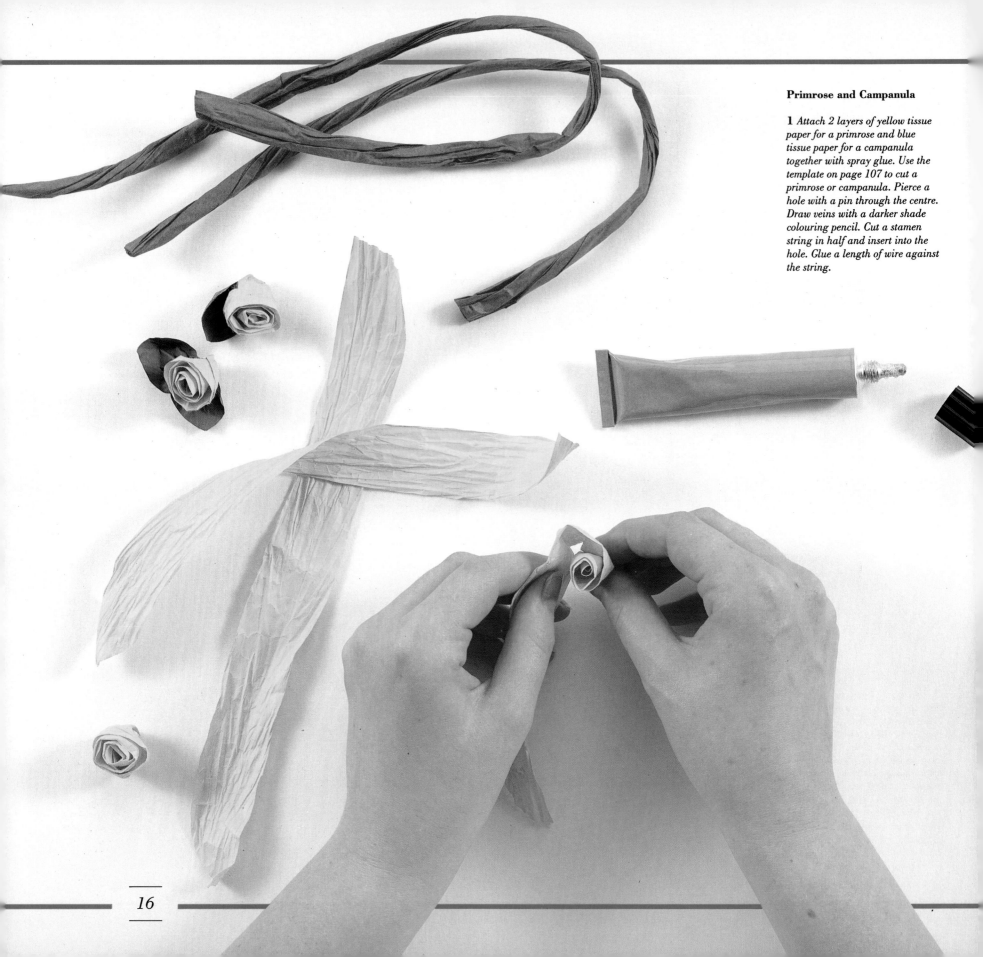

Primrose and Campanula

1 *Attach 2 layers of yellow tissue paper for a primrose and blue tissue paper for a campanula together with spray glue. Use the template on page 107 to cut a primrose or campanula. Pierce a hole with a pin through the centre. Draw veins with a darker shade colouring pencil. Cut a stamen string in half and insert into the hole. Glue a length of wire against the string.*

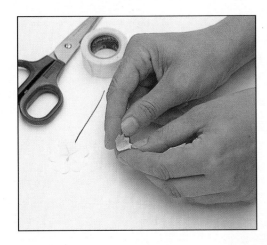

2 *Attach 2 layers of green tissue paper together with spray glue and cut out the calyx. Overlap the end points and stick together to form a cone with double-sided adhesive tape.*

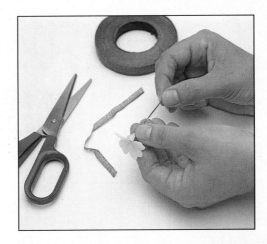

3 *Insert the wire down through the pointed base of the calyx. Trim floral tape to 6 mm (¼ in) wide. Push the calyx up against the flower so that it puckers slightly. Bind the floral tape around the base of the calyx and the stem.*

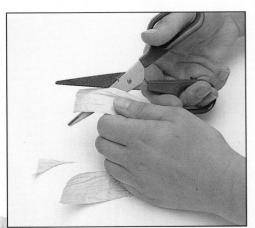

Rose

1 *Cut a strip of paper ribbon 25 x 2.8 cm (10 x 1⅛ in). Cut away the lower corners in a curve.*

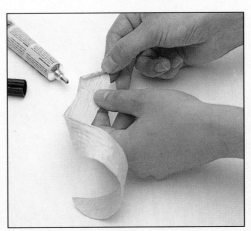

2 *Starting at one end, begin to roll up the strip keeping the lower edges level and dabbing occasionally with glue to hold in place.*

3 *Continue rolling up and gluing the rose. Make small pleats on the lower edge about 1.5 cm (⅝ in) apart so that the rose is not too tight. Cut across the lower edge so that the rose will stand upright on a flat surface.*

Topiary Tree

1 *If your pot has a hole in its base, cover the hole inside with masking tape. Following the manufacturer's instructions, pour some quick-set cement into the pot and gradually incorporate some water. When the pot is ¾ full of cement, set a wooden stick (it can be a tree branch or a length of dowelling) upright in the cement. Add more cement until its top level reaches 1 cm (⅜ in) below the rim. Leave to set.*

2 *Push a dry foam ball or cone onto the stick.*

Clematis

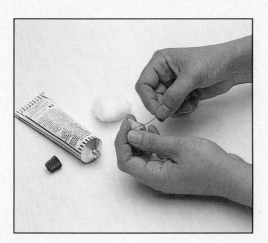

1 Bind the end of a length of wire into a hook. Wrap a ball of cotton wool around the hook for the flower centre. Cut a 3-cm (1¼ in) diameter circle of yellow crepe paper and wrap over the cotton wool. Glue the circumference to the wire.

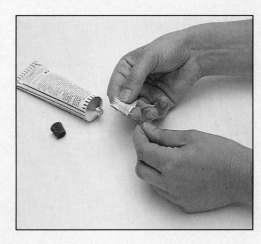

2 Cut a strip of yellow crepe paper 5 x 2.5 cm (2 x 1 in). Make fringed stamens as described on page 14. Spread glue along the lower edge and bind around the flower centre.

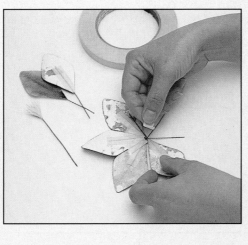

3 Use the template on page 106 to cut 6 clematis petals. Make the petals following the watercolour method on pages 12-13. Place the petals with lower edges butted together and tape together close to the pointed base on the back of the petals.

4 Insert the flower centre stem down through the middle of the petals. Bind the wires together with floral tape.

19

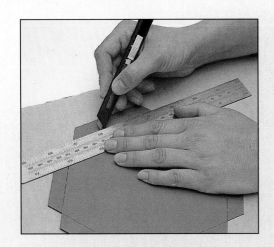

Cutting and Scoring

Cover a flat, stable surface with a cutting mat or piece of corrugated card. When cutting with a craft knife, do not press too hard or attempt to cut right through thick card at the first approach; gradually cut deeper and deeper. Always cut crepe and tissue paper with scissors rather than a craft knife to avoid tearing. If scoring, do not cut all the way through the card but break the top surface only. Cut straight lines against a steel ruler.

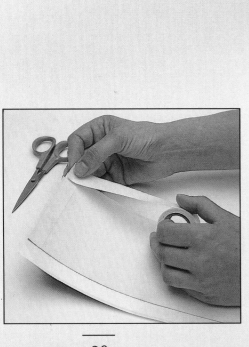

Round Box and Lid

1 *Cut a strip of card for the side of the large box 63 x 14.5 cm (25¼ x 5¾ in) or 37 x 9 cm (14¾ x 3½ in) for the small box. Apply to giftwrap or plain paper with spray glue. Trim away the excess paper around the card strip leaving an allowance of 1.5 cm (⅝ in) on the long edges. Apply double-sided adhesive tape to the allowances and one end on the wrong side.*

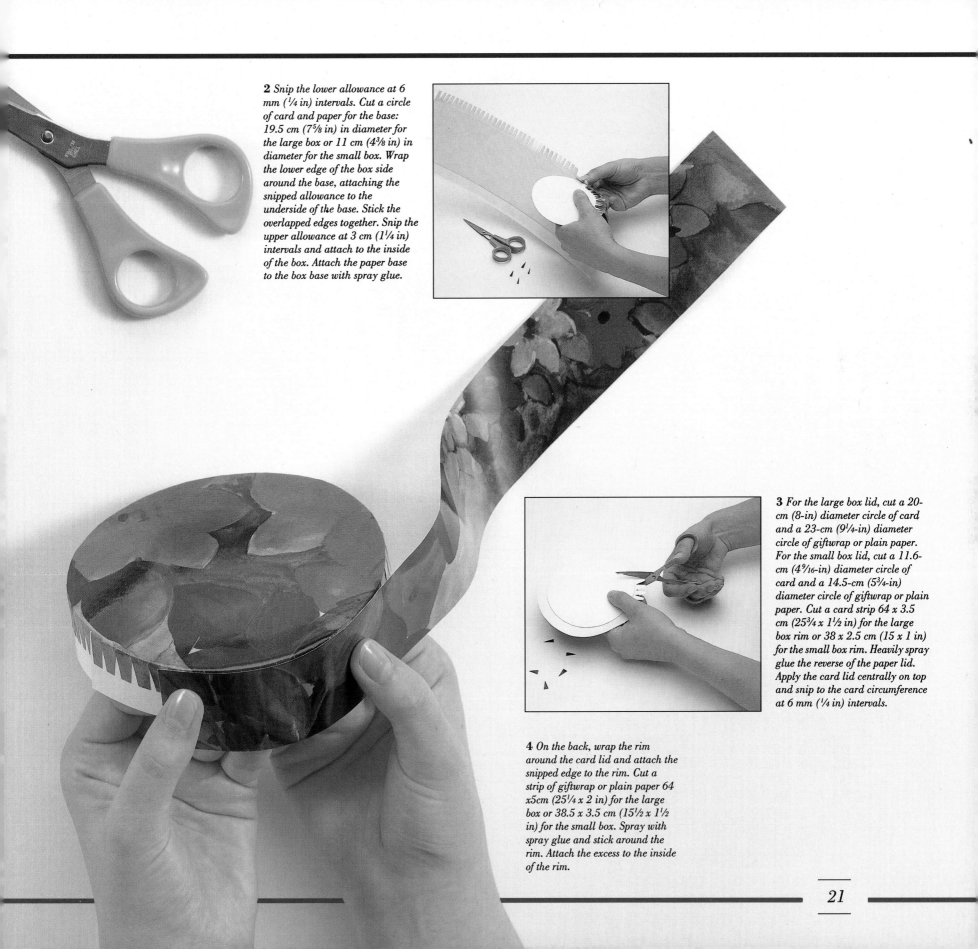

2 Snip the lower allowance at 6 mm ($\frac{1}{4}$ in) intervals. Cut a circle of card and paper for the base: 19.5 cm (7$\frac{5}{8}$ in) in diameter for the large box or 11 cm (4$\frac{3}{8}$ in) in diameter for the small box. Wrap the lower edge of the box side around the base, attaching the snipped allowance to the underside of the base. Stick the overlapped edges together. Snip the upper allowance at 3 cm (1$\frac{1}{4}$ in) intervals and attach to the inside of the box. Attach the paper base to the box base with spray glue.

3 For the large box lid, cut a 20-cm (8-in) diameter circle of card and a 23-cm (9$\frac{1}{4}$-in) diameter circle of giftwrap or plain paper. For the small box lid, cut a 11.6-cm (4$\frac{9}{16}$-in) diameter circle of card and a 14.5-cm (5$\frac{3}{4}$-in) diameter circle of giftwrap or plain paper. Cut a card strip 64 x 3.5 cm (25$\frac{3}{4}$ x 1$\frac{1}{2}$ in) for the large box rim or 38 x 2.5 cm (15 x 1 in) for the small box rim. Heavily spray glue the reverse of the paper lid. Apply the card lid centrally on top and snip to the card circumference at 6 mm ($\frac{1}{4}$ in) intervals.

4 On the back, wrap the rim around the card lid and attach the snipped edge to the rim. Cut a strip of giftwrap or plain paper 64 x5cm (25$\frac{1}{4}$ x 2 in) for the large box or 38.5 x 3.5 cm (15$\frac{1}{2}$ x 1$\frac{1}{2}$ in) for the small box. Spray with spray glue and stick around the rim. Attach the excess to the inside of the rim.

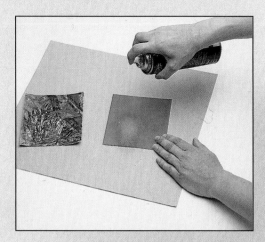

Spray Mounting

Spray gluing 2 layers of paper or card together gives a smooth, even finish. Place the surface to be sprayed in an old box or on a flat surface, protecting the surrounding area with newspaper or scrap paper. Always use a CFC-free spray glue and spray the back of the paper or card evenly following the directions on the can. Press the 2 layers together. If stuck in the wrong position, one of the layers can be lifted and replaced correctly.

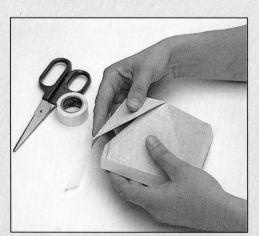

Pointed Lid

1 *Take the pointed lid and rim and score the back along the broken lines. Bend forward along the scored lines. Apply double-sided adhesive tape to the tabs on the right side. Stick the end tab under the opposite side of the lid.*

2 *Starting at the tab end, stick the lower tabs to the rim, keeping the lower edges level. Stick the opposite end over the end tab.*

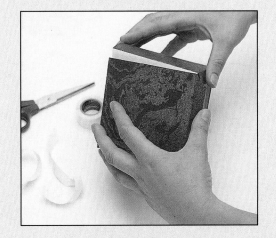

Square Box

1 *Cut the box following the diagram on page 103. Score the back along broken lines and bend forward along the scored lines. Apply double-sided adhesive tape to the tabs on the back of the base tabs and the right side of the end tab. Stick the base tab under the base.*

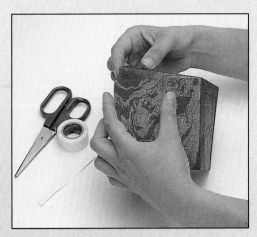

2 *Stick the end tab under the opposite end.*

Hexagonal Box

1 *Cut out following the diagram on page 104. Score the back along broken lines. Bend forward along the scored lines. Apply double-sided adhesive tape to the tabs on the right side.*

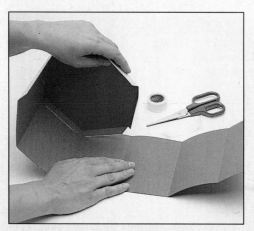

2 *Starting at the tab end, stick the base tabs under the lower edge and the end tab under the opposite end.*

Smocking

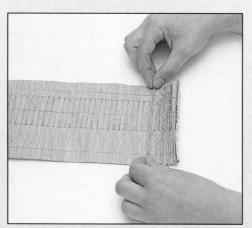

1 *Cut a length of metallic crepe paper 82.6 x 12.1 cm (32⅝ x 4¾ in). Mark a grid on the back following the diagram on page 102. On the back, fold in concertina pleats widthways folding along the first line with the wrong sides together.*

2 *Starting on the top row on the right side, bring the first and second pleats together with a small stitch using a needle and thread. Sew on a bead. Fasten off the thread securely on the back. Continue along the top row, bringing together the third and fourth pleats next.*

3 Now work the middle row in the same way starting with the second and third pleat. Work the lower row in the same order as the top row forming a diamond pattern. Join the strip together end to end with tape on the back. To finish, bring the second and last pleats together on the middle row and attach a bead.

Tissue Honeycomb

1 *Cut the motif from layers of tissue paper along the solid lines – the amount of layers needed is marked on each template. To cut through more than one layer accurately, staple the layers together first. Also, cut the motif along broken lines from card.*

2 *If you are making the fruit, score the card leaves along dotted lines. Bend backwards along the scored lines. Sew the layers together along the centre dotted line. Glue the card sections underneath.*

3 *Lift the tissue paper halves on one side except the bottom one. Dab paper glue on the bottom half close to the edge in the centre, then each side at 4 cm (1¾ in) intervals. Press down the next half and dab glue close to the edge between the first positions. Continue to the top tissue layer, alternating positions.*

4 *Glue the other half in the same way, then carefully stick the top 2 halves together. Glue the card sections together.*

A Wealth of Wreaths

Wreaths are highly decorative items that can transform any wall or door. They are a practical decoration for parties or receptions, even if they are made predominantly from paper, since they can be placed in a prominent position, high up where they will not be damaged or obscured by people. Wreaths can also be suspended by ribbon or decorative string from a ceiling. Alternatively, they can be positioned in pride of place on a table to make an eye-catching centrepiece. For a special celebratory gathering, the centre of the wreath could be filled with decoratively-wrapped sweets or miniature gifts for an extra treat.

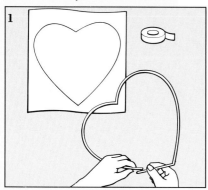

1 Draw a heart 26 cm (10¼ in) in height on paper and cut out. Use as a template to bend a length of thick wire into a heart shape. Overlap the ends and secure with masking tape.

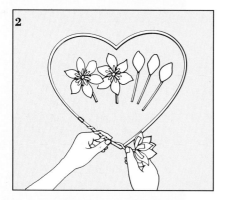

2 Make 3 clematis flowers (template on page 106) following the instructions on page 19 and about 26 leaves following the watercolour instructions on pages 12-13 using the clematis petal as a template. Bind the flowers to the wire heart base with the wire stems. Attach the leaves in the same way.

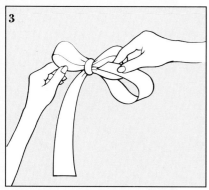

3 Bind the heart base with floral tape. To make a double bow, loosely tie a length of ribbon in a bow. Pull the ends back through the knot and pull the knot tighter. Trim the ribbon ends in a fishtail.

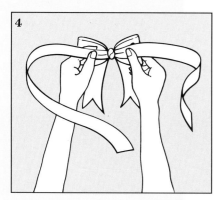

4 Thread a length of ribbon through the back of the bow and tie to the middle top of the heart.

Bend thick wire into a heart shape 26 cm (10¼ in) in height. Overlap the ends and secure with masking tape. Make 25 Himalayan poppies (template on page 106) following the instructions on pages 14-15. Make green tissue paper leaves using the template on page 106 and following the double layer method on page 13.

1 Starting at the middle top point, bind the wire stems of the poppies to the heart.

2 Attach the leaves in the same way between the poppies. Bind the heart with floral tape.

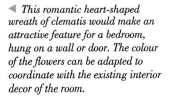 *This romantic heart-shaped wreath of clematis would make an attractive feature for a bedroom, hung on a wall or door. The colour of the flowers can be adapted to coordinate with the existing interior decor of the room.*

▲ *A stunning wreath of Himalayan poppies which would make a memorable gift for a wedding anniversary or a special birthday. The flowers are wonderfully convincing made from bright blue crepe paper.*

Using the spring and autumn leaves templates – and the 2 larger ivy templates – on page 106, and the 2 largest Virginia Creeper templates on page 115, make some leaves following the watercolour instructions on pages 12-13 in shades of green. Fold the leaves along the 'veins'.

1 Gloss varnish the leaves. Push the leaves into a dry foam ring, placing them in the same direction.

2 Add small bunches of artificial berries, pushing the stems into the ring.

▲ The vibrant colours of this evergreen ring adorned with berries will brighten the home all year round.

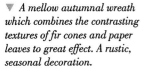

▼ *A mellow autumnal wreath which combines the contrasting textures of fir cones and paper leaves to great effect. A rustic, seasonal decoration.*

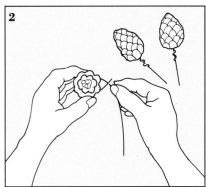

Use the spring and autumn leaves templates – and the 2 larger ivy templates on page 106 – and the Virginia Creeper template on page 115 to make leaves in brown, red, orange and ochre colours following the watercolour instructions on pages 12-13. Fold the leaves along the 'veins'.

1 *Gloss varnish some of the leaves. Push the leaves into a dry foam ring, positioning the leaves in the same direction.*

2 *Bind wire around the base of small pine cones and push into the ring at intervals in small groups.*

33

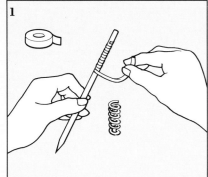

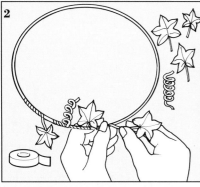

Bend thick wire into a circle 25 cm (10 in) in diameter. Overlap the ends and bind together using masking tape. Make variegated ivy leaves using the varying sizes of templates on page 106 and the watercolour instructions on pages 12-13. Paint the leaves cream, add pale green details and finally dark green areas. Fold along the 'veins'.

1 Bind wire with floral tape. Coil the wire around a pencil, then remove the pencil. Pull coil slightly open to form a tendril.

2 Bind the wire stems of the leaves around the base wire circle. Twist lengths of wire to form tendrils and bind to the wreath. Bind the base ring with floral tape to neaten and secure the leaves and tendrils in place.

1 Bind large curtain rings with narrow strips of cream paper, gluing the ends of the strips onto the backs of the rings. Use the templates on page 106 to cut small ivy leaves for the rings.

2 To make the ring with dark green leaves, bind fine wire with green floral tape and wrap around the ring. Make 5 leaves following the watercolour instructions on pages 12-13 and using dark green paint. Fold the leaves along the 'veins'. Do not attach the leaves to wires; glue directly onto the ring.

3 To make the ring with the bow, make 5 leaves following the watercolour instructions on pages 12-13. Paint the leaves bright green, then use a fine paintbrush to paint them deep red but leaving fine green lines. Trim 2 leaves smaller than the others. Do not attach the leaves to wires. Tie a bow of narrow paper ribbon and glue to the top of the ring. Glue the leaves to the ring.

4 Make 3 variegated ivy leaves referring to the watercolour instructions on pages 12-13 and to page 34. Also, refer to page 34 to make 2 tendrils. Use masking tape to secure the ends of the tendrils to the ring. Glue the leaves to the ring, covering the masking tape.

◀ *Once mastered, the painting technique required to create these variegated ivy leaves is surprisingly easy and the results are highly realistic.*

▲ *These enchanting ivy-clad rings make unusual decorations for the festive season. Small willow rings can be used in place of curtain rings to give a more rustic effect.*

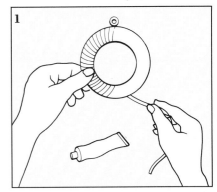

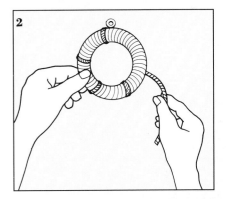

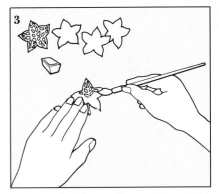

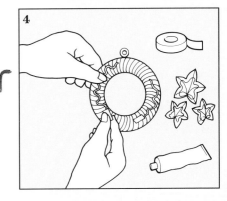

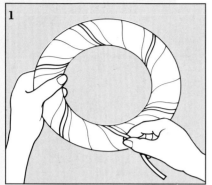

1 *Bind a polystyrene ring with strips of crepe paper, then bind with narrow giftwrapping ribbon, securing the ends to the back of the ring with adhesive.*

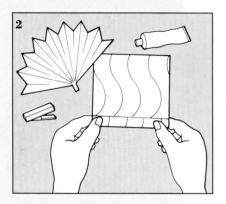

2 *Cut 2 strips of giftwrap 24 x 7 cm (10 x 2¾ in). Fold each strip widthways in concertina pleats 1.2 cm (½ in) wide. Pinch the folds together at the lower long edge of each fan and staple in place. Glue the fans to the ring.*

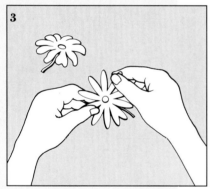

3 *Make 2 large daisies following the instructions on page 15. Curve the petals between thumb and finger.*

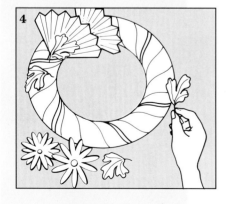

4 *Use the daisy leaf template on page 106 to make 4 leaves from green paper following the single layer method on page 13. Fold the leaves along the 'veins'. Push the daisy and leaf stems into the ring close to the fans.*

▲ *A cheerful daisy wreath that brings with it a breath of summer. Use brightly-coloured giftwrap to enhance the 3-dimensional quality of the fans.*

1 *Cut 5-cm (2-in) squares from blue tissue paper. Fold each one loosely into quarters. Insert into a dry foam ring by pushing the folded edge of each square into the ring with the blunt end of a plastic cocktail stick. Continue until the ring is covered.*

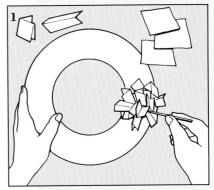

▼ *This dazzling tissue-paper nest decorated with 'hovering' butterflies provides a fun way to present small edible treats to junior birthday party guests.*

2 *Glue a circle of card to the back of the ring and fill the centre with miniature Easter eggs or sweets. Use the templates on page 107 to cut 5 upper and 5 lower butterfly parts from glossy coloured card, using the outer line in each case. Overlap the top butterfly over the lower section and glue together.*

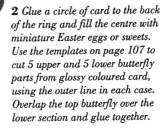

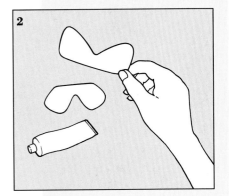

3 *Cut 5 bodies (template on page 107) from glossy black card. Glue to the butterflies positioning between the dashed guidelines on the butterfly templates.*

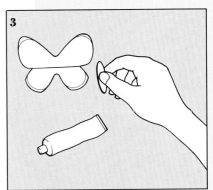

4 *Bend black stamen strings in half for the antennae. Position on the underside of each butterfly together with a length of fine wire extending downwards. Tape in place. With the butterflies face down, bend the wires upwards. Push the butterfly wires into the ring at intervals.*

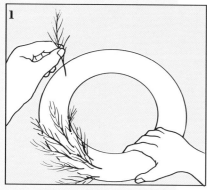

Gather together frothy dried grasses, wheat and barley in natural and yellow colourings.

1 Push the stems of the dried materials into a dry foam ring, positioning all the foliage in the same direction.

2 Make 7 field poppies following the instructions on pages 14–15. Push the poppy stems into the ring at regular intervals.

▲ As in nature, the vibrant red of these paper field poppies contrasts perfectly with the ripening yellow of the cereal grasses.

▶ Bring the natural beauty of a meadow into your home with this wreath of dried wild grasses sprinkled with dainty daisies and buttercups.

1 *Push stems of green grasses, wheat and oats into a dry foam ring, all facing the same direction.*

2 *Make 20 buttercups following the instructions on pages 14-15. Push the flower stems into the ring at random.*

3 *Make 20 small daisies following the instructions on page 15. Arrange them amongst the buttercups.*

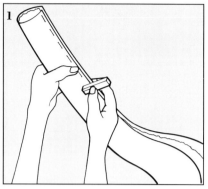

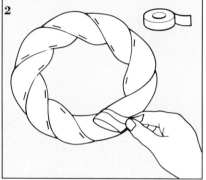

Cut 3 strips of paper ribbon 1 m x 11.5 cm (40 x 4⅝ in) for the plaited wreath and 2 strips 85 x 11.5 cm (34x 4⅝ in) for the twisted wreath. Cut 3 strips of wadding 1 m x 8.5 cm (40 x 3½ in) for the plaited wreath and 2 strips 85 x 8.5 cm (34 x 3½ in) for the twisted wreath.

1 Wrap the paper strips around the wadding. Staple the long edges together. Lightly spray with gold paint.

2 Plait or twist the strips together. Bend into a circular shape, overlap the ends and tape together, making sure the joins are at the back of the wreath.

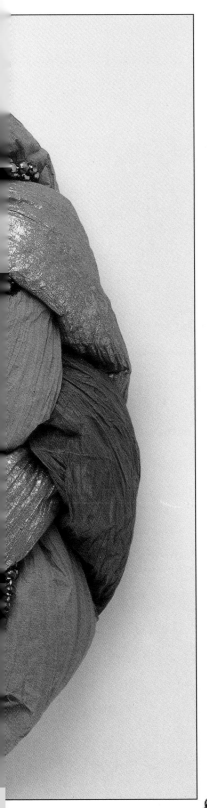

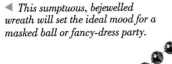 This sumptuous, bejewelled wreath will set the ideal mood for a masked ball or fancy-dress party.

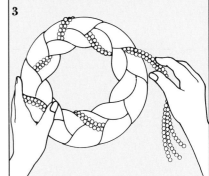

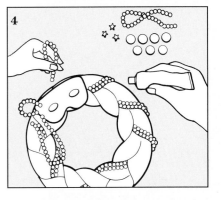

3 Thread 3 strings of beads between the plaits. Cut a mask from metallic card using the template on page 107.

4 Glue the mask to the wreath. Decorate with jewellery stones, sequin stars and strings of beads.

Use the comedy and tragedy faces from the templates on page 109 to cut 2 masks from gold card for the twisted wreath. Pull the masks between thumb and finger to curve. Cut gold card stars using the templates on page 107. Glue masks and stars to the wreath.

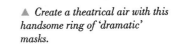 Create a theatrical air with this handsome ring of 'dramatic' masks.

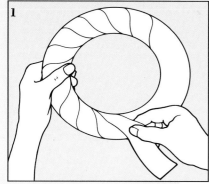

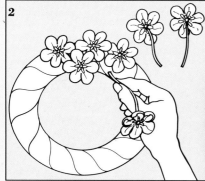

Following the instructions on pages 14-15, make anemones in pink, red and mauve crepe paper. Cut leaves from green crepe paper using the template on page 107. Make leaves using the single layer method on page 13.

1 Bind a dry foam ring with a strip of red crepe paper 3.5 cm (1½ in) wide.

2 Push the stems of the flowers into the ring, then add the leaves in between.

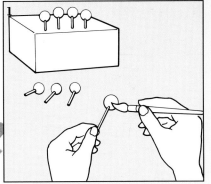

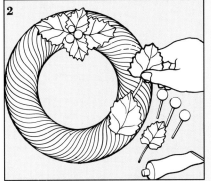

Use templates on pages 107 and 115 to cut vine leaves from 2 shades of green paper. Fold along the 'veins', then lightly spray with gold spray paint. Prepare leaves following the single layer method on page 13. To make berries, push 14 cotton pulp balls onto green covered wire.

1 Mix mauve and gold craft paints, and use to paint the balls. Push the wires into modelling clay (Plasticine) or a dry foam block to dry.

2 Spray a willow ring with gold spray paint. Dab glue along the wire stems of the leaves and berries. Push into the ring to form 3 groups.

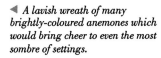 *A lavish wreath of many brightly-coloured anemones which would bring cheer to even the most sombre of settings.*

▲ *A quick and simple wreath to make, but highly effective in result. For a Christmas alternative, use silver spray paint in place of the gold.*

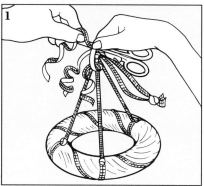

1 *Bind a willow ring with tartan giftwrapping ribbon, applying glue to the ends and pushing them into the willow. Cut 6 1-m (40-in) lengths of the tartan ribbon. Tie 3 lengths of ribbon around the ring, dividing it into thirds. Tie the free ends of the lengths of ribbon above the ring. Tie the 3 remaining lengths of ribbon around the extending ribbons 25 cm (10 in) above the knot. Pull the free ends smoothly over the back of a pair of scissors to curl them.*

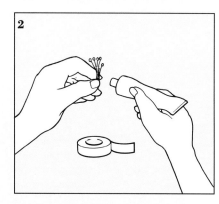

2 *Bunch together about 12 yellow stamen strings and bend in half. Dab with glue close to the fold. When the glue has dried, bind together with floral tape.*

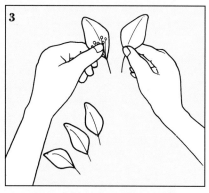

3 *To make a poinsettia flower, use the clematis template on page 106 to cut 6 petals from red paper and to make 2 leaves from green paper following the double layer method on page 13. Bind 3 petals to the stamens with floral tape, then add the remaining 3 between them. Make about 6 or 7 poinsettias and 12-14 leaves.*

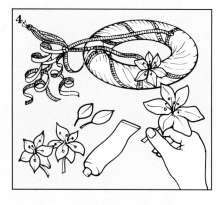

4 *Bind the wire stems of the leaves with floral tape. Dab glue onto the poinsettia stem wires and push into the ring. Dab leaf stems in the same way and position 2 leaves each side of every flower.*

▲ When hung on a door, this sparkling wreath would signal a suitably festive welcome to party guests.

◀ Surface space is often in short supply during the festive season, therefore suspending a decorated ring from the ceiling exploits a further dimension.

1 Cut metallic crepe paper 150 x 24 cm (60 x 10 in) and join the short ends together on the reverse of the paper with adhesive tape.

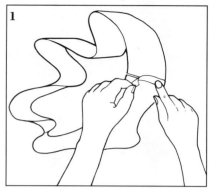

2 Place a 25-cm (10-in) diameter dry foam ring in the middle of the circle of paper. Staple the long edges of the paper together to enclose the ring, arranging the join under the ring.

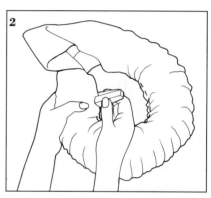

3 Wrap 4 small boxes with foil giftwrap and fasten with giftwrapping ribbon. Bend lengths of wire in half and thread through the ribbon on the underside of the boxes. Thread wire through the rings of glossy baubles in the same way.

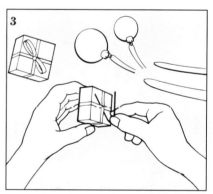

4 Arrange the boxes and larger baubles on opposite sides of the ring, pushing the wires into the ring. Make some stars from metallic card using the template on page 107 and following the single layer method on page 13. Push the wire 'stems' into the ring together with some smaller baubles. Drape a string of beads around the ring, gluing the ends on the underside.

Trees & Topiary

The adorned tree is much-loved as a traditional focal point in the home at Christmas. However, in recent times, people have begun to discover the potential that different kinds of trees and topiary offer for interior decoration throughout the year. Many of the designs presented in this chapter would make innovative and enchanting centrepieces for permanent display, while others are ingenious gift ideas for special celebrations such as Mother's Day or a wedding anniversary.

1 *Prepare the tree with a length of dowelling in a ramekin pot following step 1 of the topiary tree instructions on page 18. Scrunch green tissue paper and glue on top of the hardened cement in the pot.*

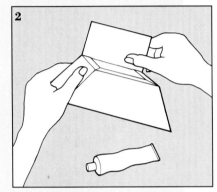

2 *Refer to the diagram on page 102 to cut dry foam blocks into 3 sections. Cover the sections with green tissue paper.*

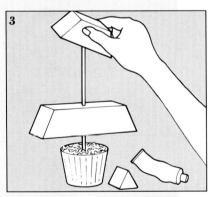

3 *Push the dowelling centrally up through the largest section, then add the middle and top sections leaving a space 5.5 cm (2¼ in) deep between each one. Dab glue around the holes to hold the sections firmly.*

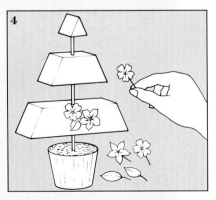

4 *Make some primroses in yellow, pink and white tissue paper, together with some campanulas in blue and mauve tissue paper following the instructions on pages 16-17. Make green tissue primrose leaves using the template on page 107 and following the double layer method on page 13. Insert the flower and leaf stems into the foam sections to cover.*

▲ *Place this pretty tree on a sunny windowsill to add life and colour to an interior.*

▶ *This delightful little tree of delicate primrose and campanula flowers would make an eye-catching centrepiece for an Easter tea party.*

1 *Follow the instructions on page 18 to prepare a tree in a pretty pot using a length of white dowelling for the trunk and a dry foam ball. Cover the ball with green tissue paper and paint the hardened cement green.*

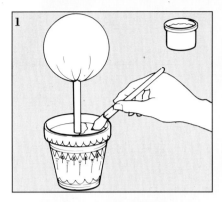

2 *Make green primrose leaves using the template on page 107 and following the double layer method on page 13. Trim away the extending wires from some of the leaves and curve the leaves between thumb and finger. Dab glue on the ends of these leaves and position on the hardened cement.*

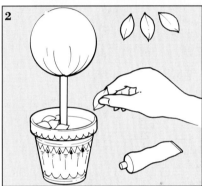

3 *Make yellow primroses and blue campanulas following the instructions on pages 16-17. Push the wire stems of the flowers and leaves into the ball.*

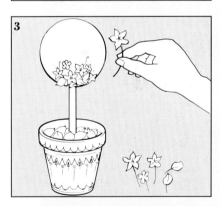

4 *Push the long wire stems of 4 leaves into the ball so that the leaves hang down close to the front of the trunk.*

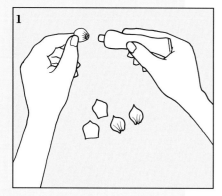

Prepare a tree in a terracotta pot following the instructions on page 18 and using a straight branch and a dry foam oasis ball. Glue moss onto the hardened cement. Make up some roses from paper ribbon following the instructions on page 17. Cut green paper ribbon rose leaves from the template on page 107.

1 Gather up the straight edges of the leaves. Dab with glue to hold the gathers.

2 Glue the roses and leaves onto the ball to cover completely.

◀ *Add floral fragrance to this ever-blooming rose tree by gluing potpourri onto the hardened cement in place of moss.*

▶ *This attractive rose ball would make a therapeutic get-well gift to hang at a bedside.*

1 *Bind a 6-mm (¼-in) wide strip of bright yellow paper ribbon around a length of coiled patterned paper ribbon. Glue in place. Pierce a hole through the end of the coiled length of ribbon. Insert a long length of wire through the hole and bend the wire ends downwards. Push the wire ends through the centre of a dry foam ball and splay the emerging ends open under the ball.*

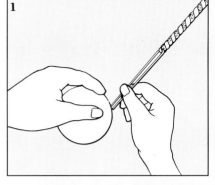

2 *Make roses from bright yellow and lemon paper ribbon following the instructions on page 17. Use the template on page 107 to cut rose leaves from 2 shades of green paper ribbon. Gather up the lower straight edges and dab with glue to hold the gathers. Glue the roses and leaves to the ball to cover completely.*

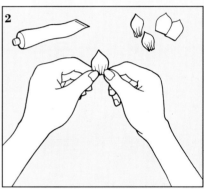

3 *To make the bow, cut a strip of patterned paper ribbon 34 x 8.5 cm (13¾ x 3¾ in). Fold in the ends to meet the middle point along the ribbon's length and overlap. Gather up the centre and bind tightly with a narrow strip of adhesive tape.*

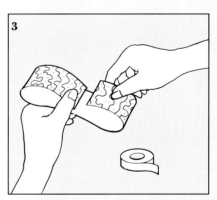

4 *Bind the centre of the bow with a strip of patterned paper to make the 'knot', gluing the ends in place at the back of the bow. Glue the bow to the top of the rose ball.*

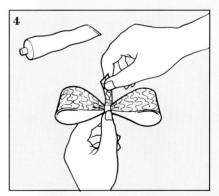

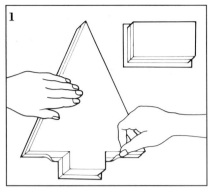

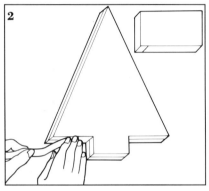

Following the diagram on page 102, cut 2 trees from 5-mm (¼-in) thick foam board and 2 rectangles for the base 13 x 7 cm (5 x 2¾ in). Glue the tree pieces together, then the base pieces, using spray glue to make one tree. For the partridge and dove trees, apply green or gold paper to both sides of the trees and the bases with spray glue.

1 Cut off excess paper leaving a 6 mm (¼ in) allowance. Wrap the allowance around the sides of the trees and the bases, snipping the corners to fit.

2 Apply double-sided adhesive tape to the back of a piece of the same paper you have used to cover the trees and cut strips 1 cm (⅜ in) wide. Apply to the sides of the trees, joining the strips if necessary.

Three unusual and stylish Christmas trees. Make decorations of your own design to hang on the map pins. The bauble tree could be covered with purple metallic crepe paper, as a vampish alternative, and teamed with silver baubles or other decorations of your choice.

3 *To cover the front of the bauble tree and the top of the base, scrunch metallic green crepe paper between your fingers and glue to the tree and base. Cut off the excess paper leaving a 6 mm (¼ in) allowance. Glue the allowance to the sides of the foam board.*

4 *Cover the tree back and underside of the bauble tree base in the same way as the green and gold trees. Neaten the sides in the same way. Glue the trees centrally onto their bases.*

5 *Push map pins into the front side of the trees at intervals. Paint the pin heads to colour coordinate if you wish.*

6 *Cut a partridge and several pears from gold card or doves from white card using the templates on page 107. Attach a loop of gold thread to the back of each decoration. Hang the shapes on the map pins, by the loops. Hang miniature glossy baubles on the bauble tree and add a star decoration to the top of the tree.*

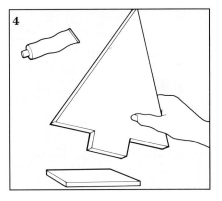

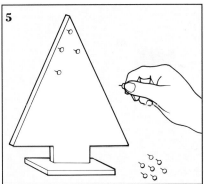

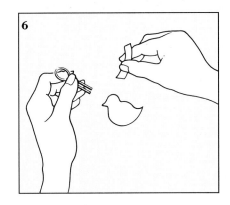

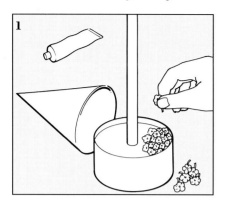

1 Paint an oval wooden box with a watery solution of poster paint. Leave to dry, then prepare the tree as shown on page 18 using a length of painted dowelling for the trunk. Glue dried flower heads to cover the cement in the box. Push a dry foam cone centrally onto the dowelling. Glue or insert dried flowers to cover the cone completely.

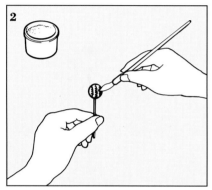

2 To make the bees, push 1.5-cm (⅝-in) diameter cotton pulp balls onto lengths of fine wire. Dab with glue to secure in place. Paint the balls yellow. Paint a black stripe around the middle of each ball, then a black circle at each end. The brushstrokes can be quite uneven to give the effect of the 'furry' texture of a bee's body.

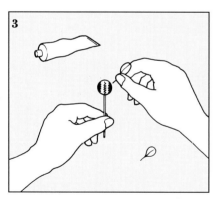

3 Use the small wing template on page 107 and follow the double layer method on page 13 to make 2 wings for each bee from white frosted paper. Trim the extending wires to 6 mm (¼ in) long. Dab the ends of the wires lightly with glue. Pierce 2 holes in the black stripe around the middle of the bee's body, on the top side. Insert a wing wire into each hole.

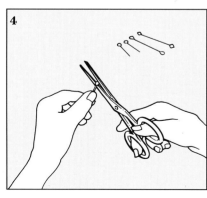

4 To make the antennae, cut black stamen strings to 1.2 cm (¼ in) below the stamens; you will need 2 for each bee. Using a small pair of scissors, carefully trim the stamens to make them slightly smaller. Pierce 2 holes on the bee's 'head' for the antennae. Dab a little glue on the ends of the strings and insert one in each hole. Insert the wire bee 'stems' at intervals into the tree. Bend the antennae upwards.

◄ This is a fun tree design with a swarm of friendly bees 'buzzing' around its delicate dried flowers.

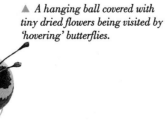

▲ A hanging ball covered with tiny dried flowers being visited by 'hovering' butterflies.

1 Bend a length of thick wire in half to resemble a hairpin. Push the ends through the centre of a dry foam ball until the top loop extends above the ball slightly. Splay open the ends of the wire under the ball. Thread ribbon through the loop and knot the free ends together. Tie a wider ribbon in a bow around the hanging ribbon.

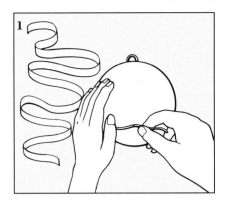

2 Glue or insert dried flowers all over the ball to cover. To make a butterfly, apply double-sided adhesive tape to the reverse of metallic blue paper. Cut a top and a lower butterfly part using the templates on page 107, following the inner line in both cases. Peel away the backing from the adhesive tape and apply the wings to black paper. Cut out the butterfly parts from the black paper but following the outer line of the templates on page 107 and matching the position of the broken lines.

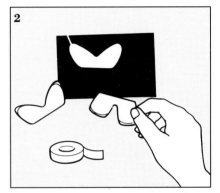

3 Overlap the top butterfly over the lower section and glue together. Cut a body from black card using the template on page 107. Glue to the butterfly between the broken guidelines. Bend the wings upwards.

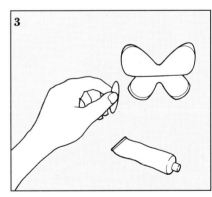

4 Bend a black stamen string in half for the antennae. Place on the reverse of the butterfly with a length of fine wire extending downwards. Tape in position. Make another butterfly in the same way. Push the butterfly wires into the ball.

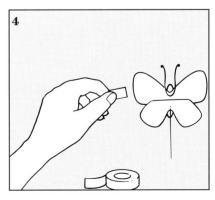

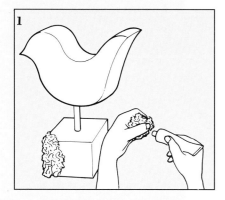

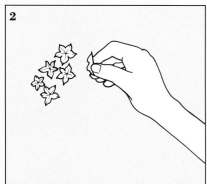

Glue 2 dry foam blocks together. Use the template on page 108 to cut the topiary bird from the foam. Cut a rectangle 9 cm (3½ in) wide and 7 cm (2¾ in) high from foam for the base. Insert a 9-cm (3½-in) long tree branch centrally into the base to stand upright. Push the bird on top.

1 Scrunch textured green paper. Glue to the model. Cut dark green paper leaves using the smallest ivy leaf template on page 106.

2 Trim some leaves smaller. Fold along the 'veins'. Glue to the model, trailing upwards from the base.

◀ *A stylized bird is a traditional motif in the formal garden art of topiary. Our version would make an unusual and elegant decoration for a windowsill. A vine of real small-leaved ivy could be trailed in a circle around the base of the bird.*

▶ *This evergreen arch decked with roses makes a perfect frame for a pair of period china figurines.*

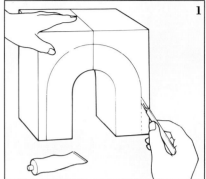

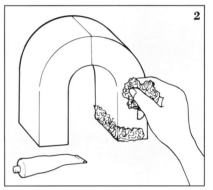

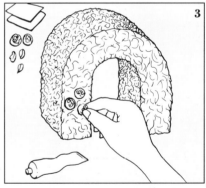

1 *Glue together 2 dry foam blocks. Cut an archway, judging the height and shape in relation to your figurines.*

2 *Scrunch textured green paper and glue to the model. Cut tiny leaves from green paper and fold in half.*

3 *Cut 3.5 cm (1½ in) orange tissue paper squares. Scrunch into balls and glue to the arch with the leaves.*

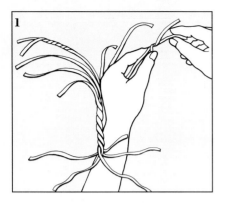

1 *Take 5 lengths of bonsai tree wire. Splay open the ends for tree roots, then twist the wires together to form a trunk. Open out the wire ends to create branches. Add extra branches by twisting the ends around the trunk.*

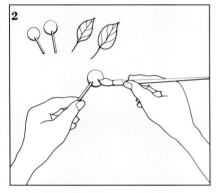

2 *Push 2.5-cm (1-in) diameter cotton pulp balls onto green covered wire. Paint the balls orange. Use the template on page 107 to make leaves from green paper using the double layer method on page 13. Fold the leaves along the centre and down the 'veins'.*

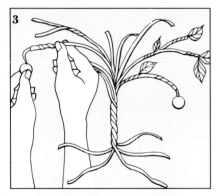

3 *Attach the oranges and leaves to the branches by twisting the wire 'stems' together.*

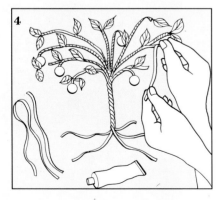

4 *Spread glue on the back of narrow strips of paper and bind around the wires. Paint the trunk, branches and roots brown.*

▲ *Alternative fruit trees can be created, such as cherry and plum trees, using different-shaped leaves, smaller balls and different-coloured paints for the fruit. Additionally, the bonsai wire can be used to create a bush rather than a tree, upon which can be hung blackcurrants or redcurrants.*

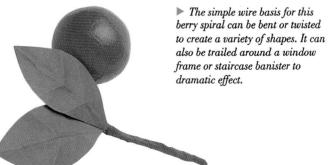

▶ *The simple wire basis for this berry spiral can be bent or twisted to create a variety of shapes. It can also be trailed around a window frame or staircase banister to dramatic effect.*

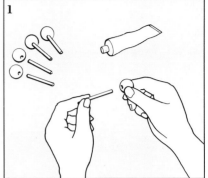

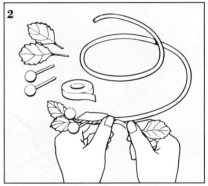

Twist thick wire upwards in a spiral. Use the template on page 107 to make berry leaves following the double layer method on page 13 and using dark green paper for the top and light green for the underside. Fold the leaves along the centre and the 'veins'.

1 Push 2-cm (¾-in) diameter cotton pulp balls onto green covered wire. Paint the balls violet with poster paints.

2 Bind the leaf and berry wires around the spiral. Bind with floral tape to secure in place.

59

Boxed Beautifully

Practical or ornamental, this collection of colourful containers caters for all tastes. There are heart-shaped boxes for the romantic, floral designs for the nature lover, as well as fun and novelty ideas for the young and the young at heart. The containers can be used for storing treasured items of jewellery or personal keepsakes. Alternatively, boxes can be tailor-made to house special gifts for family and friends.

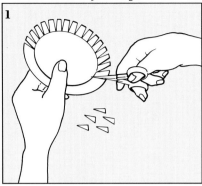

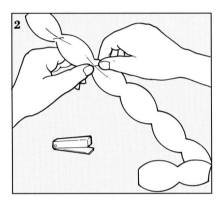

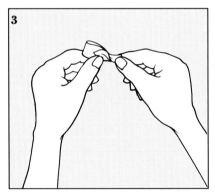

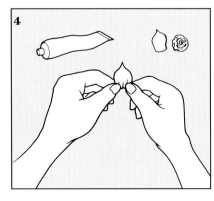

1 *Follow the instructions on pages 20-21, steps 1 and 2, to make a small, round cream box. For the lid, cut a 10.6-cm (4¼-in) diameter circle of card and a 14.5-cm (5¾-in) diameter circle of cream paper. Cut a strip of card and cream paper 38 x 1.5 cm (15 x ⅝ in). Spray the back of the paper circle heavily with spray glue. Position the card circle centrally on the paper and snip the paper to the card at 6 mm (¼ in) intervals.*

2 *On the wrong side, wrap the card strip around the card circle, sticking the snipped circumference to the outside of the strip. Spray glue the back of the paper strip and apply to the rim. Cut 2.5-cm (1-in) wide yellow blotting paper strips 40.5 cm (16 in) long for the lid and 38.6 cm (15½ in) for the base. Divide strips into eighths. Cut scallops along the long edges. Make small pleats at the divisions and staple in place. Glue around lid and bottom of the base.*

3 *Place lid on the box. Wrap a length of turquoise ribbon around the box, securing ends with double-sided adhesive tape. Saw balsa wood dowelling 8 cm (3¼ in) long and paint turquoise. Make a hole in the centre top with an awl. Glue bottom of dowelling to the centre of the lid. To make the flame, fold a red foil sweet wrapper into a triangle. Fold a yellow cellophane sweet wrapper over the triangle and twist lower edges together. Cut cellophane into a flame shape.*

4 *Push the twisted end of the flame into the dowelling hole. Cut 17 strips of white blotting paper 18 x 2 cm (7¼ x ¾ in). Cut off lower corners in a curve. Dampen the strips and make roses following the instructions on page 17, steps 2 and 3, omitting the glue. Cut 2 rose leaves from yellow blotting paper using the template on page 107. Gather straight edges together and glue in front of the candle with one rose. Glue remaining roses to scalloped strips covering staples.*

◄ *This celebration cake container would make a fun memento to mark a friend's birthday, especially if the recipient is on a reduced-calorie diet! Alternatively, it could be used to prettily package a piece of wedding cake for a sadly-missed guest.*

▼ *This bead-encrusted box with its matching earrings employs a technique usually associated with embroidery, but the honeycomb effect of smocking works surprisingly well with sturdy papers.*

1 *Make a small, round box and lid following the instructions on pages 20-21 using plain paper to cover the box. Refer to the smocking instructions on pages 24-25 to make a smocked panel of gold crepe paper. Slip the panel over the box with allowances extending at the top and lower edges. Attach the allowances under the base and inside the top of the box with double-sided adhesive tape.*

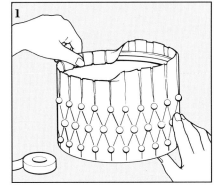

2 *Cut a crepe paper strip for the lid 37 x 11.5 cm (14⅝ x 4½ in). To reinforce the long upper edge, apply clear adhesive tape on the reverse along the edge. Fold under 1.5 cm (⅝ in) along this edge. Apply 2.5-cm (1-in) wide double-sided adhesive tape along the lower edge and stick to the lid with 1.5 cm (⅝ in) extending below the rim. Secure the overlapping short edges together with double-sided adhesive tape. Stick the extending lower edge inside the lid.*

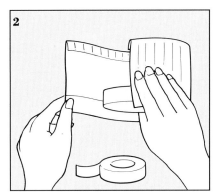

3 *Gather folded edge with needle and thread. Carefully pull up gathers tightly. Fasten thread at the centre. To make a tassel, cut a strip of gold crepe paper 12.5 x 7 cm (5 x 2¾ in), then cut a fringe along one long edge. Roll up strip and fasten a needle and thread to the top. Thread on a cup-shaped jewellery finding, 2 tiny beads then a large bead. Insert needle through lid centre and fasten thread inside.*

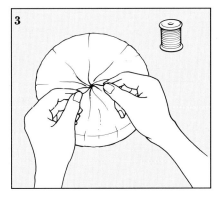

4 *To make earrings, thread beads onto headpins, bending the top into a loop with pliers. Tie loops together with fine wire. Thread the wire through a cup-shaped jewellery finding, through a jumpring and back through the cup. Dab strong glue inside the cup to secure the wire. Attach to earring hooks.*

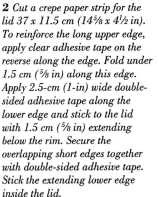

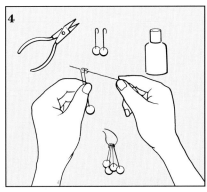

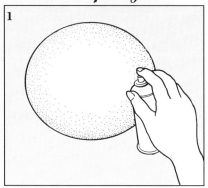

1 *Refer to the instructions on pages 20-21 to make a large, round box and lid. Use deep pink paper to cover the box and lid. Spray the lower half of the box side, lid rim and circumference of the circle for the lid with blue spray paint.*

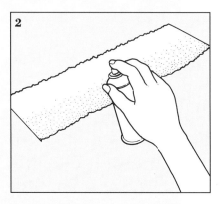

2 *Referring to the poppy instructions on pages 14-15, make 4 flower centres from green paper ribbon. Add green paper ribbon stamen fringes to 2 of the centres. Cut 8-cm (3¼-in) wide strips of pink, deep pink and mauve crepe paper. Lightly spray the lower long edges with blue spray paint. Use the poppy petal template on page 106 to cut 6 pink, 6 deep pink and 12 mauve petals from the crepe paper. Stretch the petals widthways.*

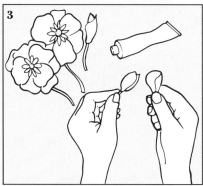

3 *Glue 3 pink petals then 3 deep pink petals and finally 4 mauve petals to each fringed flower centre. To make buds, glue a mauve petal around each of the remaining flower centres, then glue a second mauve petal around the first on each bud.*

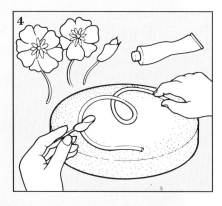

4 *Bind narrow strips of green paper ribbon around the flower and bud stems. Cut a 45-cm (18-in) length of coiled green paper ribbon. Arrange on the box lid with the flowers and buds. Glue the flowers and buds in position, then the paper ribbon.*

▲ *These round boxes are both attractive and practical. Make a range in different papers and sizes to hold treasured letters, keepsakes or items of jewellery.*

◀ *Have fun experimenting with colourful crepe papers to make alternative fantasy-style flowers in various sizes, shapes and hues.*

1 *Follow the instructions on pages 22-23 to make a large, round box and lid covered with striped paper. Cut 2 strips of crepe paper 4 cm (1½ in) wide and one strip 7.5 cm (3 in) wide. Cut the paper with the ends parallel with the grain of the paper. Spray the long edges lightly with spray paint. Stretch the long edges between thumb and finger.*

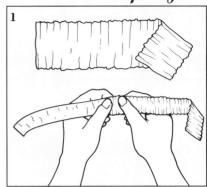

2 *Place the narrow strips across the top of the lid and secure the ends inside on the underside of the lid with double-sided adhesive tape. To make the bow, trim one wide strip to 35 cm (14 in) in length. Fold the ends into the centre. Make concertina pleats widthways at the centre.*

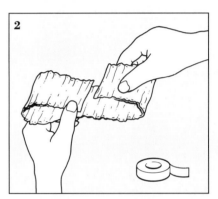

3 *Cut the remaining wide strip 17 cm (7 in) long. Fold in concertina pleats across the centre. Hold the strip against the back of the bow, matching centres, and bind together with a narrow strip of crepe paper. Glue the ends at the back of the bow.*

4 *Trim the bow 'tails' into a fishtail shape. Glue the bow to the narrow crepe paper strip on the lid. The photograph also shows a small, round box covered with giftwrap, which can be made by following the instructions on pages 20-21.*

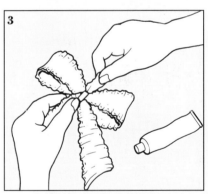

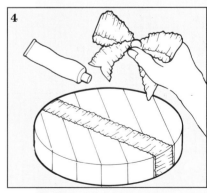

Boxed Beautifully

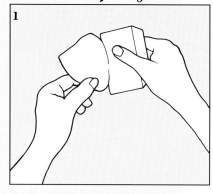

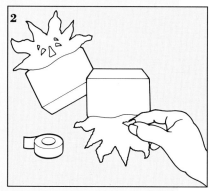

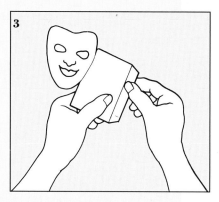

From card covered with marbled paper, make 3 square boxes following the instructions on pages 22-23. Use the templates on pages 108-109 to cut 2 leaf lids from gold card, 2 sun lids from yellow card (outline only – do not cut out features) and 2 mask lids from orange card. Score the right side along the broken and dashed lines.

1 Pull the sun and masks between finger and thumb to curve the card.

2 Spray glue 2 layers of yellow card together. Back with double-sided adhesive tape. Cut out the sun facial features, using the template, and stick in position on the sun.

Cut out the comedy face on one mask and the tragedy face on the other.

3 Fold the lids backwards along the broken lines and forwards along the dashed lines.

4 Use double-sided adhesive tape to attach the tabs to the inside upper edge of the box on opposite sides.

▶ All the giftboxes in this glamorous collection are made using the same simple method, then topped with lids of varying designs. Look out for colourful and unusually-patterned papers to cover your own leaf, mask and sun boxes.

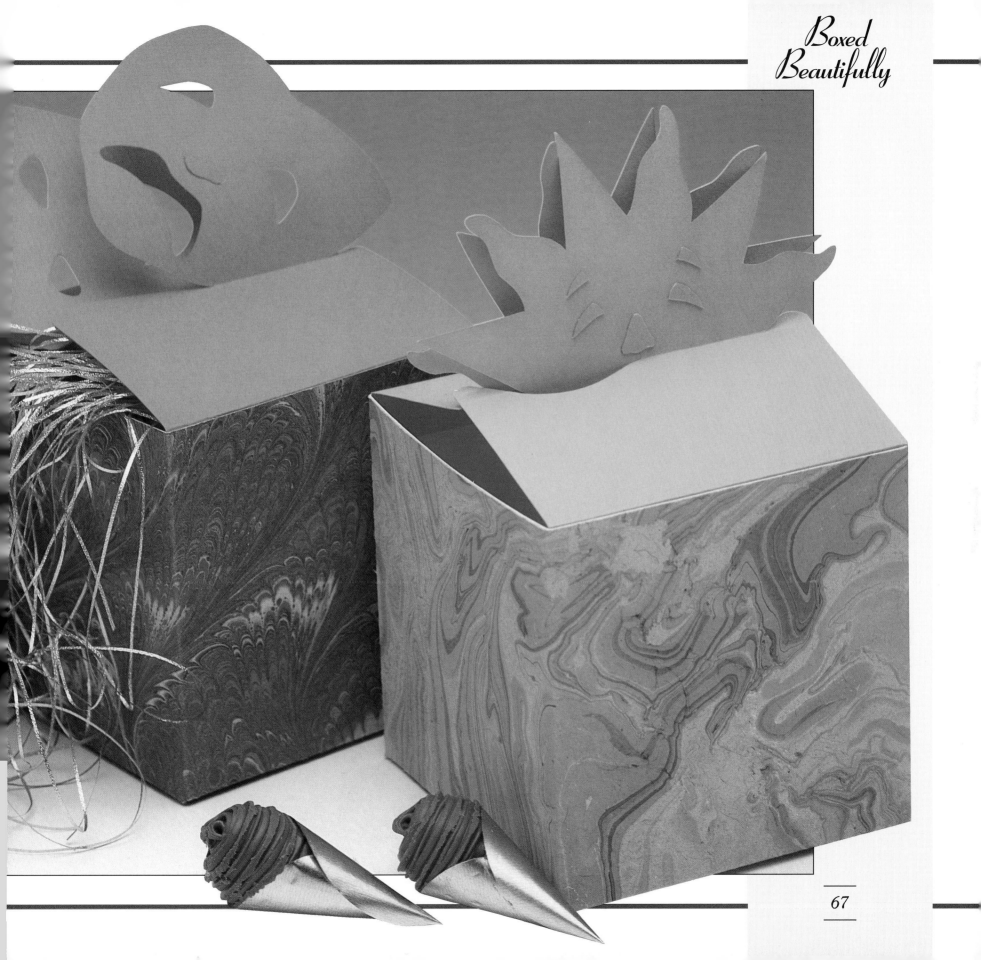

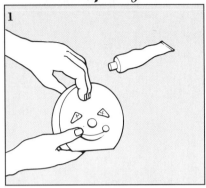

1 *Use the template on page 110 to cut 2 clowns from pale pink card and the facial features from plain giftwrap backed with double-sided adhesive tape. Position the features on one clown head. Score the back of the clown along the broken lines and fold forwards along the scored lines. Glue the clown heads together at the top.*

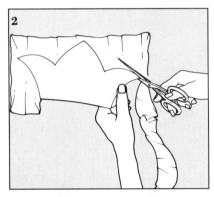

2 *Glue lengths of curled giftwrapping ribbon to either side of the face as hair. Cut 2 hats from card using the template on page 109 and apply to crepe paper with spray glue. Trim away the crepe paper around the card hats. Apply plain giftwrap to a piece of card with spray glue. Cut 2 hat rims and 3 stars from the covered card. Glue a rim to each of the hats.*

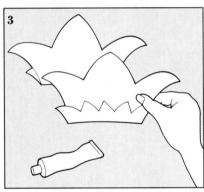

3 *Glue the hats together around the edges, leaving the lower edges open. Slip the hat over the clown's head. Glue the stars to the points of the hat. Make a hexagonal box from card covered with a patterned giftwrap following the instructions on page 24.*

4 *Cut another box base (template on page 111) from card covered with plain giftwrap for the lid. Score the back along the broken lines and bend forward along the scored lines. Glue the base of the clown centrally onto the lid. Glue one tab of the lid to the inside upper edge of one side of the box.*

◀ *This jolly clown box would make a fine gift for an older child, for storing stationery or small toys.*

▼ *All the fun of the fair! This carousel, with its galloping horses, can be decorated as simply or as lavishly as you wish. Add ribbons and feathers to create a truly flamboyant effect.*

1 *Apply giftwrap in 3 colourways to card with spray glue. Make a hexagonal box following the instructions on page 24 in one colourway. Cut a pointed hexagonal lid from the second colourway and the carousel rim from the remaining card using the template and diagram on pages 111 and 103 respectively. Cover the lower half of the rim with newspaper, then lightly spray the top half with gold spray paint.*

2 *Make the lid following the instructions on page 24. Apply narrow giftwrapping ribbon to the lower edge. Cut a flag from metallic paper. Glue the end around a cocktail stick cut in half. Push the stick through the point of the lid.*

3 *Cut 3 8.5-cm (3½-in) and 3 7-cm (2¾-in) lengths of painted dowelling. Bind with narrow giftwrapping ribbon and glue the ends in place. Glue one piece of dowelling centrally to each side of the box, alternating the 2 different lengths. Keep the upper edges level.*

4 *Use the template on page 110 to cut 6 horses from card. Fringe the mane and tail, then fold the mane over to the right side. Cut saddles from giftwrap covered card and glue to the horses. Cut giftwrapping ribbon into strips 3 mm (⅛ in) wide and glue across the horses' heads as shown in the photograph. Glue a horse to each of the pieces of dowelling. Decorate the carousel with tiny sequin and paper stars.*

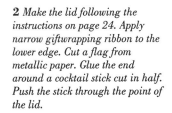

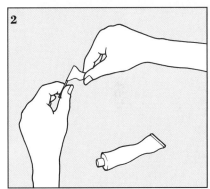

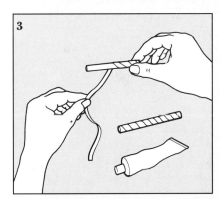

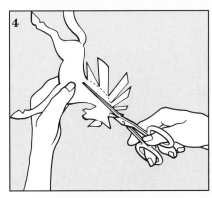

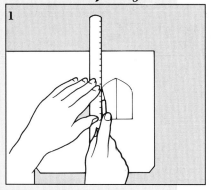

1 *Refer to the square box and square pointed lid rim diagrams on pages 103 and 105 respectively to cut a box and rim along the tall box line from thin textured pink card. Use the template on page 111 to draw a window on each box side. Cut along the solid lines and score along the broken lines.*

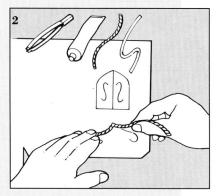

2 *Lightly draw simple curled designs on the box sides, windows and lid rim. Cut 3-mm (⅛-in) wide strips of card and trim the ends diagonally. Hold the strips at one end and twist them from the other end. Carefully dab a little glue on the drawn design and press the twisted strip in place. Trim the other ends diagonally. A pair of tweezers are useful for holding the twisted strips in place.*

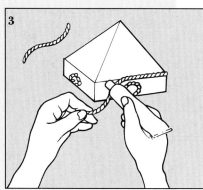

3 *Cut a square pointed lid from card using the template on page 112. Make the box and lid following instructions on pages 22-23. Apply twisted paper strips as above along the edges of the rim. Use the templates on page 111 to make about 6 dove bodies from white textured card following the double layer method on page 13. Cut a slit in the bodies along the solid line.*

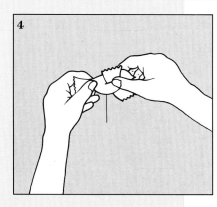

4 *Apply white textured card back to back with spray glue and cut wings for each bird (template also on page 111). Score along the broken lines. Insert the wings into the body slits and bend the wings upwards. To attach the doves to the lid, pierce a hole in the card with a pin. Insert the dove's wire into the hole and glue in place. Open the windows and position some doves so that they appear to be flying out.*

▲ *This highly decorative flower-covered box would look dramatically sophisticated made entirely of white materials.*

◄ *As a variation on the dovecot theme, make this box from gold-coloured card with bluebirds cut from metallic blue card.*

1 *From pale green card, cut out a square box using the diagram on page 103 and a square pointed lid using the template on page 112. Refer to the diagram on page 105 to cut a square pointed lid rim from white card. Apply double-sided adhesive tape to the back of white card and cut long strips 6 mm (¼ in) wide. Apply diagonally to the sides of the box and lid in a criss-cross pattern, trimming the strips level with the base and edges of the lid.*

2 *Make up the box and lid following the instructions on pages 22-23. Cut a strip of white card 41.5 x 1.2 cm (16⅜ x ½ in) and attach to the lower edge of the box with double-sided adhesive tape.*

3 *Glue a white wooden bead to the point of the lid. Apply 2 layers of dark green tissue paper together with spray glue. Cut a large number of tiny leaves from the paper and fold them in half.*

4 *Cut 3.5-cm (1½-in) squares of bright pink tissue. Scrunch into balls and glue to the box and lid, together with the leaves, as roses.*

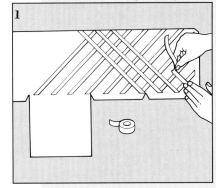

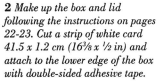
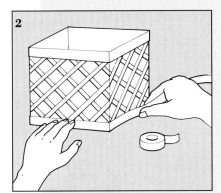

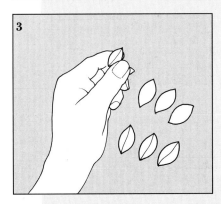

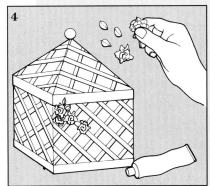

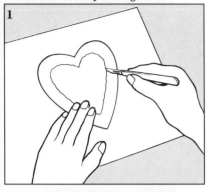

1 Using the template on page 110, cut out a large heart for the base from thick handmade paper. Also cut a heart for the lid adding 1 mm ($^1/_{16}$ in) to the circumference. Cut out the inside of the heart lid along the wavy line.

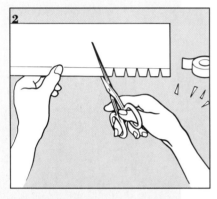

2 Refer to the diagram on page 104 to cut out the large heart box side and rim. Cut a wavy edge along the lower edge of the rim. Score along the broken lines on the wrong side and bend the tabs forwards at right angles. Apply double-sided adhesive tape to the tabs on the right side, then snip the lower and upper tabs to the scored line at 7 mm ($^5/_{16}$ in) intervals.

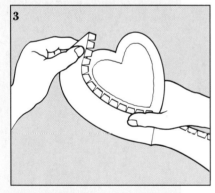

3 With the point of the heart matched to the centre fold, attach the lower tabs of the box side to the base and the upper tabs of the rim to the underside of the lid. With both the box side and the rim, stick the end tabs under the opposite ends.

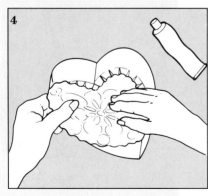

4 Paint a doily in a coordinating colour. Leave to dry, then cut a heart to fit inside the lid. Glue to the underside of the lid so that the doily pattern fills the cut-out heart on the lid. Fill the box with potpourri.

◀ *The fine filigree on the lid of this heart-shaped, subtly-coloured box filled with potpourri allows the heady fragrance to filter into the atmosphere of your home.*

▲ *This trio of miniature heart-shaped boxes is ideal for storing rings, cuff-links or earrings — or for presenting precious gifts.*

1 *Use thick paper for the boxes or apply giftwrap to thin card with spray glue. For the bases, cut out 3 small hearts using the template on page 110. Also cut out 3 hearts for the lids, adding 1 mm (¹⁄₁₆ in) to the circumference in each case. For the beaded box lid, cut out a tiny heart along the solid lines using the template on page 110. Score along the broken line and lift each side upwards. Glue a piece of contrasting paper on the reverse of each half of the heart.*

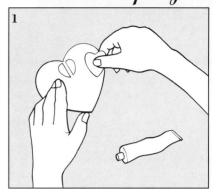

2 *Refer to the diagram on page 105 to cut out 3 small heart box sides and rims. Score along the broken lines on the wrong side and bend the tabs forwards at right angles. Apply double-sided adhesive tape to the tabs on the right side, then snip the lower and upper tabs to the scored lines at 7 mm (⁵⁄₁₆ in) intervals.*

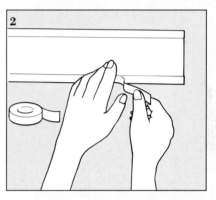

3 *Matching the points of the hearts to the centre folds, attach the lower tabs of the boxes' sides to the bases and the upper tabs of the rims to the undersides of the lids. Stick the end tabs under the opposite ends. Carefully glue sequins and small beads to the tiny heart of the beaded box, then at random to the lid.*

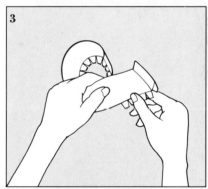

4 *Cut a dragonfly body from reptile skin effect paper using the template on page 112. Cut an upper and lower wing from green card and irridescent film. Attach each irridescent wing to a card wing at the centre with double-sided adhesive tape. Glue the wings together and the body centrally on top. Use a piece of adhesive foam to attach the dragonfly to the box lid.*

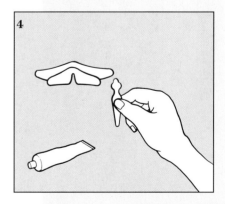

Table Taste

Entertaining at home is the occasion for indulging in dramatic effects. It is suprisingly easy to create a theme, and in this chapter there are imaginative ideas for a variety of sociable moods - from elegant intimacy to fun and frivolities. From a children's birthday party to a formal celebration banquet, here you will find the inspiration to create memorable table displays for a wide range of occasions.

Table Taste

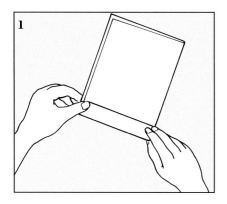

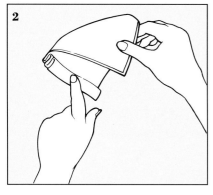

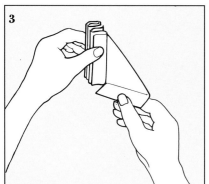

▶ *Creatively-folded napkins add a touch of class to a dining table. Here is a selection of paper trimmings to enhance table settings. Adapt the ideas to suit your own colour scheme or subject/seasonal theme.*

1 *Fold the napkins in half widthways. Fold one end back and forth widthways in concertina pleats until just past the halfway point.*

2 *Fold the napkin in half down the centre with the pleats outermost. Fold the loose ends diagonally across the unpleated area.*

3 *Fold the loose ends under the straight folded edge to support the napkin. Release the pleats so that they fall in a fan shape.*

4 *Following the instructions on page 19, make a mauve clematis. Place in front of a fan-pleated napkin.*

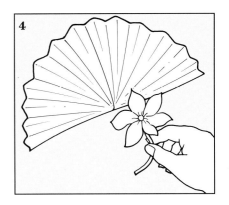

5 *To make the spray of Easter primroses, refer to the instructions on pages 16-17 to make 9 bright yellow and lemon primroses. Make some green tissue leaves following the double layer method on page 13 and using the template on page 107. Bind the stems with floral tape. Arrange in an attractive display and tie together with fine ribbons. Place in front of a fan-shaped folded napkin.*

6 *Make some tissue paper plums from the template on page 112 and following instructions on pages 26-27. Arrange on a plate with a shocking pink fan-shaped folded napkin and some grapes or lychees.*

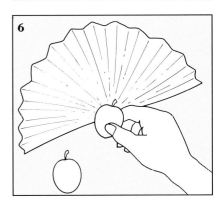

7 *For a Christmas table setting, use the template on page 112 to cut 3 holly leaves. Paint the leaves yellow, then the central area dark green. Fold each leaf in half and prepare the leaves following the single layer method on page 13. Gloss varnish the leaves, then bind the stems together with floral tape. Bend the stems backwards. Arrange with a napkin and some small fresh fruits – cranberries or cherries.*

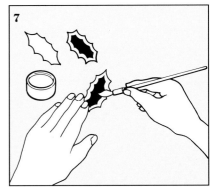

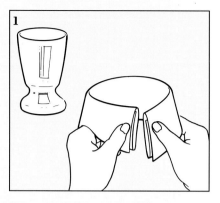

1 *Fold a napkin into a strip 6.5 cm (2½ in) wide, roll up loosely and place in the top of a glass. Apply double-sided adhesive tape to the back of silver card and cut a shallow curve for a cap brim. Attach the straight edge to the glass rim. Use the template on page 112 to cut a moustache from black card. Apply a piece of double-sided adhesive tape to the reverse of the moustache.*

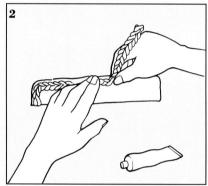

2 *Attach a second piece of double-sided adhesive tape over the first and attach the moustache to the glass below the cap brim. Cut a strip of metallic green card 3 cm (1¼ in) wide. Wrap around the base and trim to meet end to end. Cut the upper corners of the 'collar' ends in a curve. Plait gold giftwrapping ribbons together and glue to the outer edges. Attach the ends of the collar together on the reverse with clear adhesive tape.*

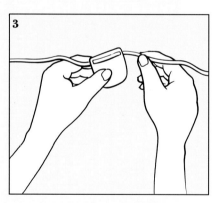

3 *Use the template on page 112 to cut an eye patch from black card. Pierce holes at the dots shown on the template and thread with black hat elastic. Tie the elastic around the glass leaving the ends long enough to tie around a head.*

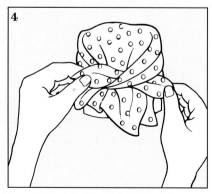

4 *Fold a spotted napkin diagonally in half. Place over the top of the glass with the fold at the front. Tie the folded ends together behind the glass. Place some chocolate gold coins beside the glass.*

▲ *Here are some amusing glass trimmings for a fancy-dress party. The jaunty pirate's eye patch and the military man's stern moustache can be removed and worn by party guests.*

▶ *This rustic poppy and grass spray would make a delightful decoration for a glass at an alfresco luncheon, while the gold ivy-clad glass is destined for a dinner of high sophistication.*

1 *To make the poppy trimmed glass, fan-pleat a patterned napkin following the instructions on page 76. Place in a tall-stemmed glass. Make a red field poppy following the instructions on pages 14-15. Bunch together some green dried grasses and bind behind the poppy with floral tape.*

2 *Divide the grasses into thirds and bend one third to one side. Dab glue on the 'bend' to hold and place in the glass.*

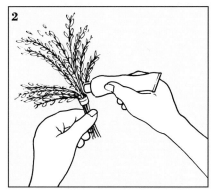

3 *For the golden ivy glass, apply small rectangles of gold paper backed with double-sided adhesive tape to the rim at intervals. Take some brass picture wire and separate the individual strands of wire. Use to make gold paper leaves, together with the 2 smaller ivy leaf templates on page 106, following the instructions for the double layer method on page 13. Fold the leaves backwards along the 'veins'.*

4 *Cut a length of brass picture wire. To make tendrils, wind each end tightly around a pencil. Remove the pencil and pull the coils apart slightly. Wrap the wire around the glass, then bind the leaf stems to this main wire.*

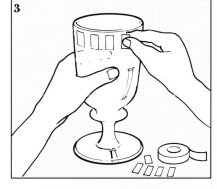

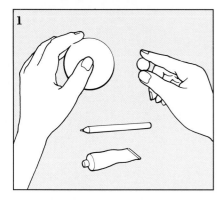

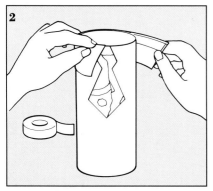

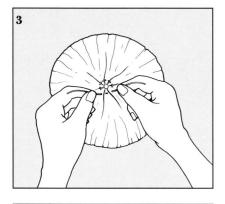

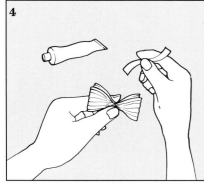

1 *Paint 2-cm (¾-in) diameter cotton pulp balls for noses and glue to 7-cm (2¾-in) diameter polystyrene balls. Draw smiling mouths with a red pen. Cut out eyes from coloured paper and attach with double-sided adhesive tape. Glue curled giftwrapping ribbon to either side of the heads. Cut coasters from coloured card (template on page 113). Place under glass tumblers as shoes.*

2 *Cut pointed hats from crepe paper (template on page 113). Overlap straight edges and glue. Turn up lower edge on one hat to create a rim. To make a crown, cut a crepe paper strip. Cut points along one long edge, overlap ends and glue. Glue hats on heads. Cut a tie from patterned giftwrap (template on page 113). Cut a collar from coloured paper and attach to glass with double-sided adhesive tape, along with the tie.*

3 *Cut a crepe paper strip 50 x 7.5 cm (20 x 3 in) for the frill. Overlap the ends and gather one long edge tightly with a needle and thread. Fasten the ends securely and place the frill on top of the glass. Cut 2 card circles for large buttons and draw details. Attach to glass with double-sided tape. Cut braces and 4 small buttons from coloured paper (template on page 112). Attach buttons to braces, then braces to glass with double-sided tape.*

4 *Cut 2 strips of crepe paper 9 x 4 cm (3½ x 1½ in) for bow-tie and 4 strips 5 x 3 cm (2 x 1¼ in) for shoe bows. Place strips together in pairs and bind a narrow strip of crepe paper tightly around centre of each pair. Secure in place. Glue pompoms to one coaster and coloured paper stars to another.*

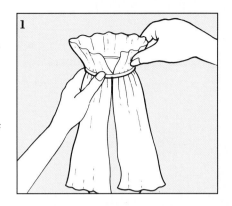

1 *Cut crepe paper for the cloaks 30 x 17.5 cm (12 x 7 in) making sure that the grain is parallel with the short edges. Stretch the long edges to flute them. Wrap the cloaks around highball glasses. Slip an elastic band around the neck of each glass. Spread the cloaks evenly under the bands. Cut the devil's tail from red paper using the template on page 112 and slip it under the glass.*

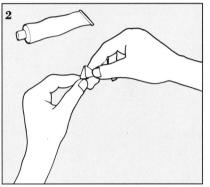

2 *Using the template on page 113, cut 3 noses from coloured paper, fold the tabs backwards along the broken lines and overlap them. Glue together, then glue each nose to a 7-cm (2¾-in) polystyrene ball. Cut out 3 mouths from coloured gummed paper. Use the templates on page 112 to cut 3 pairs of eyes from gummed paper, as well as fangs for the vampire. Draw pupils on the eyes with a felt-tipped pen. Attach features to the balls.*

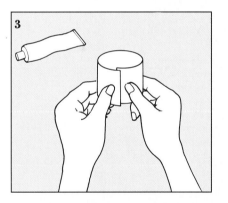

3 *Glue curled giftwrapping ribbon around the witch's face. Cut 2 hat brims (template on page 113) from card covered with gummed paper for the vampire and witch. Cut a strip of card for the vampire's hat 19 x 5.5 cm (7½ x 2¼ in). Overlap the ends and glue together.*

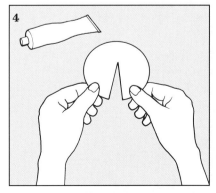

4 *From the templates on page 113, cut the pointed hat and 2 horns from coloured or gummed paper. Overlap the straight edges and glue together. Spread glue inside the lower edge of the horns and the witch's and the vampire's hats. Press the horns to the devil's head and the hats on their brims. Glue sequin stars to the witch's face and hat. Place the hats on the heads.*

◀ *Clowning around! A comical group that is sure to break the ice when used to serve liquid refreshments at a party.*

▲ *What's your poison? This spooky gathering of 'dressed to kill' glasses promise to contain potent Halloween cocktails.*

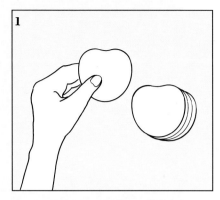

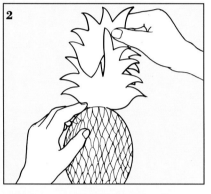

These fruits are made from tissue and card; templates on pages 112-113, 114-115. Make a pineapple from orange tissue and green card, lemons from lemon tissue and green card, plums from mauve tissue and brown card, apples from red, yellow and green tissue and green card; pears from yellow and green tissue and brown card.

1 Make the fruits following the tissue honeycomb method on pages 26-27. Mix the different coloured tissue papers on the apple and pear.

2 Cut a separate pineapple leaf from green card and cut along the slit. Slot the 2 leaves together.

▲ Here is a crop of colourful fruits, each item of which is made using the same simple technique. Make a variety of different fruits or a group of the same type to create a dramatic impact, for instance a plateful of lemons presented on a green tablecloth.

▶ These wine cooler covers offer a novel way to dress up plain wine coolers for both red and white wine. The combination of richly-coloured grapes against a gold background echoes the colour scheme of the paintings of the old Italian masters.

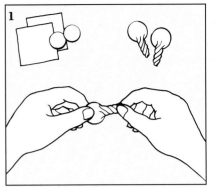

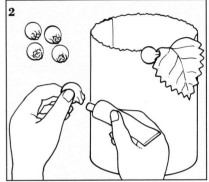

Cut a card strip to wrap around a wine cooler. Cut a wavy edge along the top. Overlap the ends and glue together. Use the templates on pages 107 or 115 to cut 2 small or 1 large green paper vine leaves. Dab gold paint close to the base of the leaves. Fold along the 'veins'. Glue to the cover.

1 *Wrap squares of mauve or green tissue paper over cotton pulp balls and twist the ends. Dab glue on the twists to secure. Cut off twists.*

2 *Gloss varnish grapes. Scrunch tissue paper into an oval to form a moulded base for the grapes. Glue to the cover and glue grapes on top.*

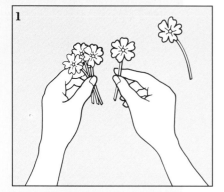

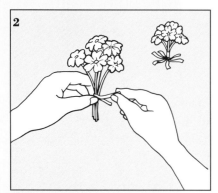

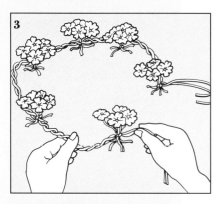

1 *Make 36 primroses in shades of orange following the instructions on pages 16-17. Bunch together in posies of 6 flowers.*

2 *Bind floral tape around the posy stems, then splay open the ends of the stems so that the flowers stand upright.*

3 *Knot twisted narrow ribbons around the posies to form a circle.*

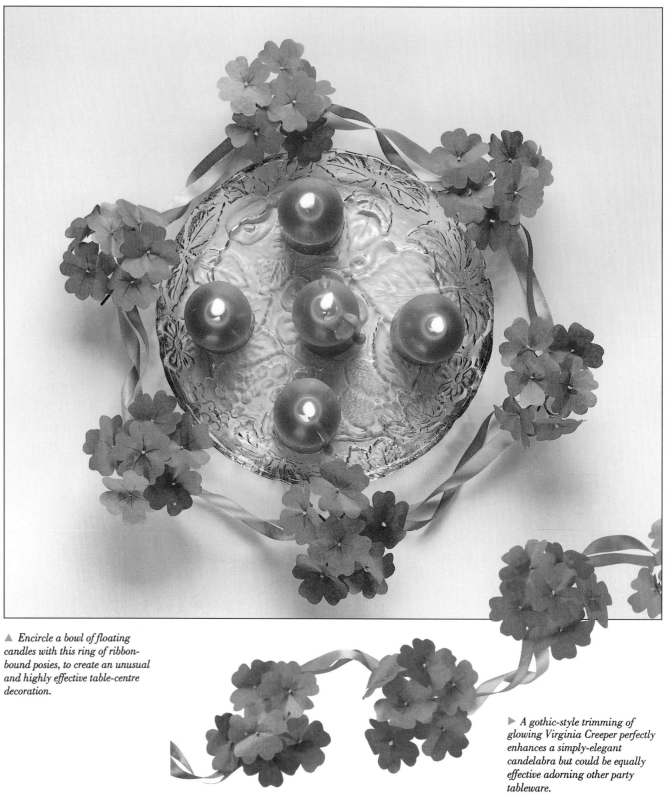

▲ *Encircle a bowl of floating candles with this ring of ribbon-bound posies, to create an unusual and highly effective table-centre decoration.*

▶ *A gothic-style trimming of glowing Virginia Creeper perfectly enhances a simply-elegant candelabra but could be equally effective adorning other party tableware.*

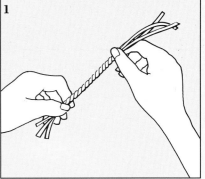

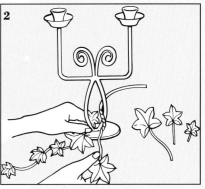

Use the Virginia Creeper leaf templates on page 115 to make some leaves in shades of orange following the watercolour method on pages 12-13. Fold the leaves backwards along the 'veins'. Fix the leaves onto fine copper wire. Trim some of the leaves smaller than the others.

1 Twist a few lengths of the wire together to make a stronger length.

2 Starting at the base, wrap the thicker wire around the candelabra, binding the leaf wires to it at intervals.

85

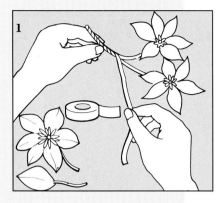

1 *Make 6 clematis on long stems following the instructions on page 19. Make 6 leaves following the watercolour method on pages 12-13 and using the clematis petal as a template. Bind together in a spray with floral tape.*

2 *Bend the wire ends to form a hook. To make a double bow, fasten 5-cm (2-in) wide ribbon in a loose bow. Pull the ends back through the knot, then pull the knot tight. Trim the ribbon ends in a fishtail shape. Thread 2.5-cm (1-in) wide ribbon through the hook. Twist the ribbon and drape it around the table.*

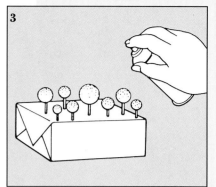

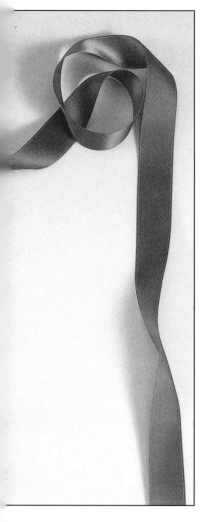

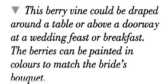
◀ *This beautiful clematis garland would be the crowning glory of a celebration meal-table, such as a Christening tea or wedding anniversary supper.*

▼ *This berry vine could be draped around a table or above a doorway at a wedding feast or breakfast. The berries can be painted in colours to match the bride's bouquet.*

3 *To make the berries, push cotton pulp balls onto lengths of green covered wire. Paint the balls pink. Push the wire into modelling clay (Plasticine) or a dry foam block covered with paper to dry. Use the templates on pages 107 and 115 to cut vine leaves from 2 shades of green paper. Fold the leaves down the centre and along the 'veins'. Lightly spray the balls and leaves with gold paint.*

4 *Prepare the leaves following the single layer method on page 13. Bind the leaves and bunches of berries to a length of string with floral tape.*

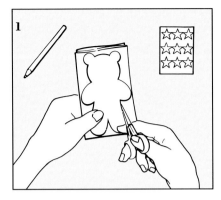

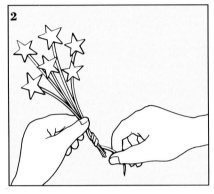

1 *Cut strips of yellow paper 10 cm (4 in) wide. Fold into concertina pleats 7 cm (2¾ in) deep. Use the template on page 115 to draw a teddy on top. Cut out through all the thicknesses, but do not cut along the folds. Open out the teddies and draw a face on each with a felt-tipped pen. Attach self-adhesive stars to the bodies. Join the strips on the back with masking tape.*

2 *Cut 6 wires 15 cm (6 in) in length. Cut narrow strips of crepe paper, spread with glue and bind around the wires. Use the template on page 107 to cut 6 metallic card stars. Attach the stars to the ends of the wires and bunch together. Bind the end of one wire around the other stems. Drape the bear garlands around the table with the bunches of stars between 2 paws.*

▲ *This garland of terrific teddies clutching stems of stars is an ideal decoration for a children's tea party table.*

▶ *Create an ocean-going theme when serving an exotic seafood supper by draping the dining table with this garland of sparkling starfish.*

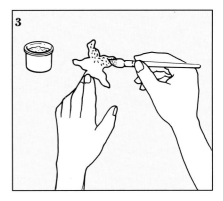

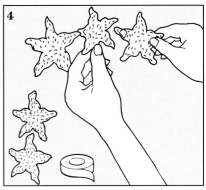

3 *To make the starfish garland, use the template on page 116 to cut starfishes from green and blue metallic card. Dab the shapes with glitter paint and leave to dry. Lightly spray with gold spray paint.*

4 *Attach the starfishes together, tip to tip in a row, with double-sided adhesive tape. Drape giftwrapping ribbon and narrow strips of irridescent crinkle film around the garland. Drape the garlands around a tablecloth and lightly catch in place with a sewing thread.*

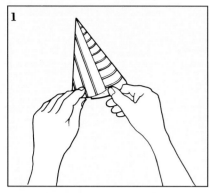

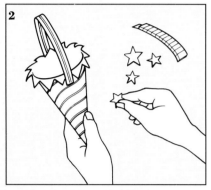

1 *Cut a semi-circle of wallpaper 28 cm (11 in) in diameter. Bend into a cone, overlapping the straight edges, and glue in place.*

2 *Cut several semi-circles of tissue paper the same size. Cut curved edges into points. Bend into a cone shape and slip inside the card cone.*

Attach 2 lengths of wallpaper 28 x 1.2 cm (11 x ½ in) together back to back with double-sided adhesive tape. Apply the ends to either side of the cone to form a handle. Cut stars from glossy pink card using the template on page 107 and attach to the cone with small pieces of adhesive foam.

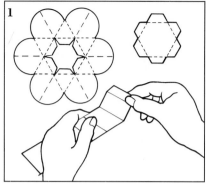

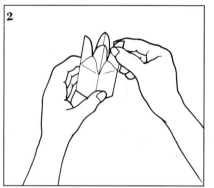

Attach 2 pieces of handmade or patterned paper together with spray glue. Using the templates on page 116, cut out the lid and base. Refer to the diagram on page 105 to cut out the box side. Score the right side along the broken and dashed lines.

1 Bend the scored lines backwards along the broken lines and forward along the dashed lines. Make the box following the hexagonal box instructions on

2 Glue lid tabs inside the top of the box. To close, squeeze 'petals' in half and fold one over the next.

◄ *This star-trimmed favour cone is a novel way to present a slice of celebration cake or petit four. The cone can be lined with coloured tissue-paper, as shown, or a lacy doily.*

▲ *These hexagonal favour boxes can be filled with dainty confections or miniature gifts to give to your guests at the end of a celebration meal.*

Crafty Creatures

Animals are always a popular subject, and these 3-dimensional paper creatures are guaranteed to appeal to the young and old alike. These are ingenious models to be recreated as unusual gifts to delight friends and family. With a little imagination, the designs can be adapted to make other real and mythical creatures.

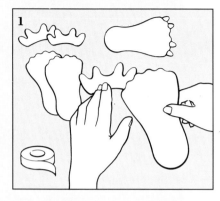

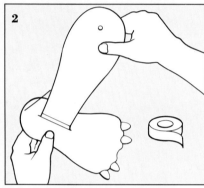

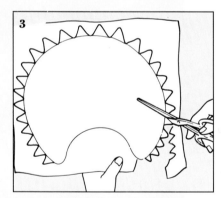

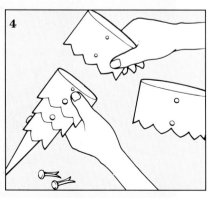

1 *Paint a piece of paper and the top of 29 brass paper fasteners with silver paint. Apply marbled paper to thick card with spray glue. Use the templates on page 117 to cut 4 feet, 2 back legs and 2 front legs. Cut 4 sets of nails from the painted paper and attach to the underside of the feet with double-sided adhesive tape.*

2 *Cut the feet slits. Score the backs of the legs along the broken lines. Fold the legs in half lengthways, attaching the tabs together with double-sided adhesive tape. Bend leg tabs at right angles and insert tabs through the foot slits. Secure in place under the feet with double-sided adhesive tape.*

3 *Apply marbled paper to coloured paper with spray glue. Use the templates on pages 117 and 118-119 to cut the tail and body sections 1-14. Pierce holes at the dots. Cut an inner collar (template on page 117) from marbled paper, glue coloured paper to the reverse and cut out along the outer collar line. Pierce holes at the dots on the legs and collar.*

4 *Stick tabs on the tail and body sections under the opposite sides with double-sided adhesive tape. Slip the tail into the first section, matching holes. Insert a brass paper fastener through the holes, opening the prongs inside. Insert the first section into the second section and attach with paper fasteners through the holes. Continue attaching sections together in numerical order adding back legs to the eighth section, front legs to the eleventh section and collar to the thirteenth section. Slip a length of thick wire through the body. Glue one end under the tail and bend the other upwards to lift the neck. Snip the wire 1 cm (⅜ in) above the last section.*

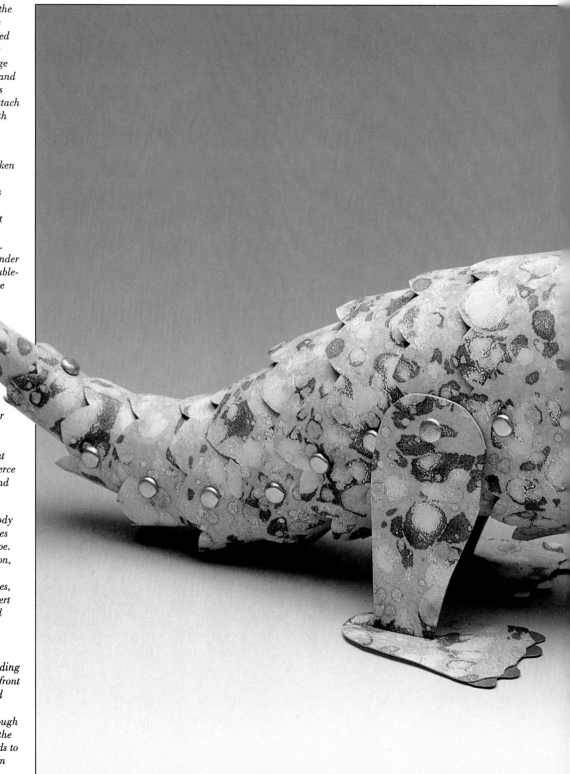

This fine fellow is a tricertops dinosaur. Study illustrations of other prehistoric monsters and adapt this basic method to make a group of these magnificent creatures.

5 *Apply marbled paper to coloured paper with spray glue. Use the templates on pages 116-117 to cut 2 heads, 2 jaws and a gusset. Cut off the nose tab on one head and jaw tab on one jaw. Score along the broken lines on the back of all pieces. Bend forward along the scored lines. Apply double-sided adhesive tape to the tabs on the right side. Snip tabs at 6 mm (¼ in) intervals.*

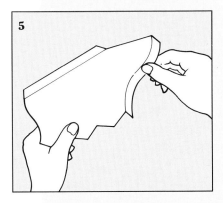

6 *Cut out the nostrils on the heads and glue grey paper underneath. Stick head tabs under the heads, matching broken lines. Cut 2 eyes from grey paper. Pierce a hole at the dots on the eyes, heads and jaws. Insert the stalk of a 6 mm (¼ in) toy safety eye through the paper eye then the head. Repeat with a second eye on the other head. Secure on the back of the heads with washers.*

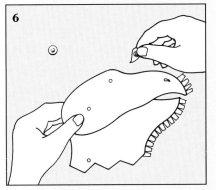

7 *Stick the nose tabs under the other head. Use the templates on pages 116-117 to cut 1 horn and 2 antlers from coloured paper. Fold the horn in half. Stick the horn tabs between the heads close to the nose with double-sided adhesive tape.*

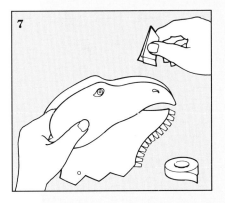

8 *Cut slits on the gusset. Matching the point to the nose, stick the gusset tabs between the heads. Slip the head over the last body section matching the holes. Fix together with paper fasteners. Stick the jaw tab under the other jaw. Bend the antlers in half lengthways and insert the tabs through the slits in the gusset. Bend the antler points and collar edge downwards.*

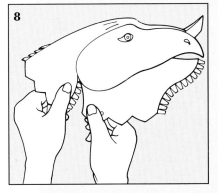

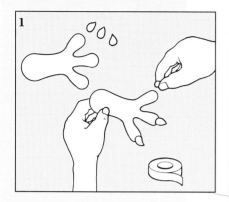

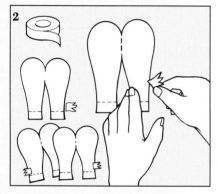

Apply 2 pieces of gold paper back to back with spray glue. Cut 2 wings, an arrow, 4 sets of nails, and leg tufts for front and back legs using the templates on pages 117, 118-119 and 120. Tape the arrow to a length of wire. Lightly spray red textured paper with gold spray paint. Apply to thick card with spray glue.

1 Cut 2 back legs, 2 front legs (page 117) and 4 feet (page 119). Attach the nails to the feet with double-sided adhesive tape.

2 Attach tufts to the backs of the legs with double-sided adhesive tape. Prepare leg following the dinosaur step 2 on page 94.

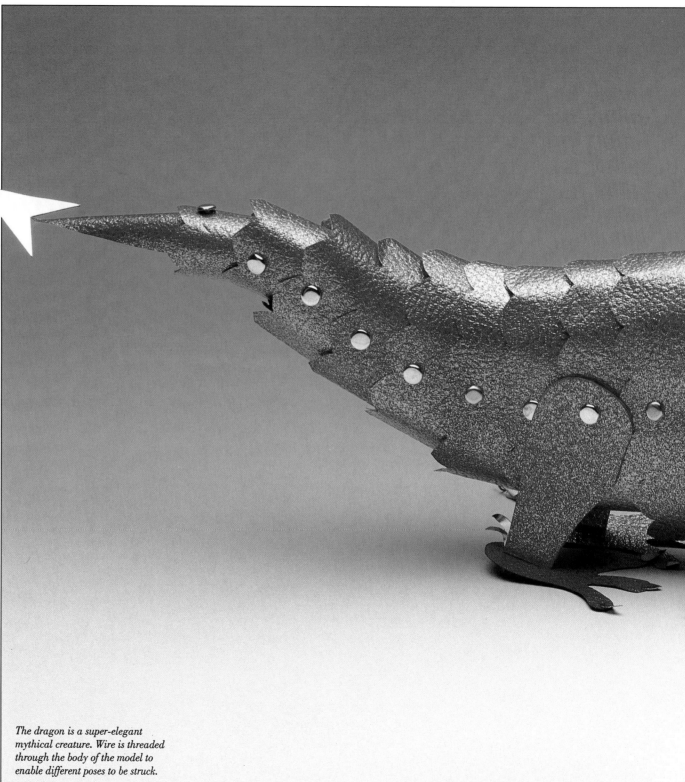

The dragon is a super-elegant mythical creature. Wire is threaded through the body of the model to enable different poses to be struck.

3 *Apply gold sprayed paper to gold paper with spray glue. Use templates on pages 117 and 118-119 to cut body sections 1-17 and the tail. Stick the arrow wire under the tail point. Fold wings along the broken lines. Pierce holes at the dots on all pieces. Attach tail and body sections together following the dinosaur step 4, attaching wings at the collar position. Using the templates on pages 118 and 120, cut a head, a jaw and a muzzle from sprayed gold backed paper.*

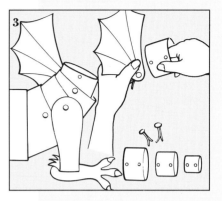

4 *Cut slits on the head and cut off one lower tab. Score the backs along broken lines. Bend bridge backwards along scored broken lines and other tabs forward along scored broken lines. Apply 2 pieces of gold paper back to back with spray glue. Cut 1 set of front teeth, 2 sets of upper teeth, 2 sets of lower teeth, 2 nostrils, 2 eyes and 2 fins. Stick teeth under heads and muzzle with double-sided adhesive tape.*

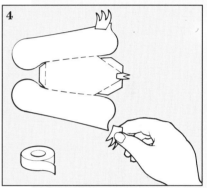

5 *Apply double-sided adhesive tape to the bridge and tabs on the right side. Snip tabs at 3 mm (⅛ in) intervals. On the head, stick the lower tab under the opposite side, then stick the jaw tabs between the lower edges matching crosses. Stick the front and back tabs between the front and back edges. Take the muzzle and stick the nose tabs to the nose between dotted lines.*

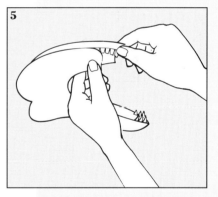

6 *Glue nostrils to the muzzle and eyes to the head. Bend eyelashes outwards. Apply double-sided adhesive tape to metallic red paper. Cut eyeballs and stick to the eyes. Pierce holes on the head at dots. Slip the head over the last body section, matching holes, and fix together with paper fasteners. Slip the muzzle into the head and stick the bridge under the straight edge. Fold fins along broken lines and insert into head slits.*

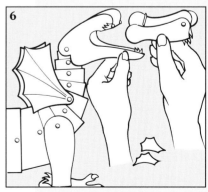

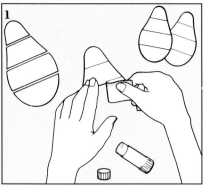

1 *Use the templates on page 121 to cut 46 bumble bee heads and middles from black tissue paper and 46 fronts and ends from yellow tissue paper. Cut 2 complete bees from yellow card. Overlap each head and middle over the fronts and ends by 4 mm (⁵/₃₂ in) and attach with paper glue. Make the bee following the tissue honeycomb instructions, steps 2-4, on pages 26-27.*

◄► *Hung from the ceiling, this hovering bumble bee is a friendly visitor to any room. The ladybird templates could be reduced in size to create a group of different-sized creatures for a children's bedroom-wall display.*

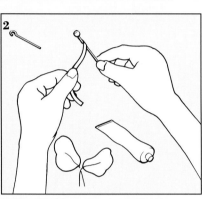

2 *Using the template on page 120, make a pair of large wings from frosted paper following the double layer method on page 13. Bend the ends of 2 lengths of wire into loops for the antennae. Cut narrow strips of black crepe paper, spread with glue and bind around the wire. Dab the extending wing and antennae wire with glue and insert into the sections on the bee. Hang the bee on a length of thread.*

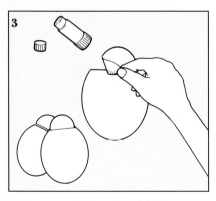

3 *Using the templates on page 120, cut 22 ladybird heads from black tissue paper and 22 bodies from red tissue paper. Cut 1 complete ladybird from red card. Overlap each head over each body by 4 mm (⁵/₃₂ in) and attach with paper glue. Sew the layers together along the central dashed line. Glue the card ladybird underneath. Make up the ladybird following step 3 of the tissue honeycomb instructions on pages 26-27.*

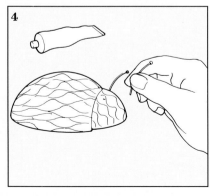

4 *Glue the other half in the same way, then carefully stick the 2 top halves together. To make the antennae, bend the ends of 2 lengths of wire into loops. Cut narrow strips of black crepe paper, spread with glue and bind around the wire. Dab the ends with glue and insert into the head sections. Glue 7 black paper circles to the body at intervals.*

▼ *This humorous caterpillar, its body sections threaded through with wire, can be bent into a variety of amusing shapes.*

1 *To make the head, tear tissue paper into small pieces. Apply to a 7-cm (2¾-in) polystyrene ball with PVA adhesive. Overlap the tissue edges to completely cover the ball. Refer to the template on page 120 to cut about 135 caterpillar sections in 5 shades of tissue paper. Staple layers of tissue together so that several sections can be cut at once.*

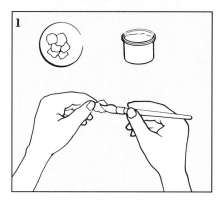

2 *Dab paper glue onto alternate scallops of the first section. Press the second section on top. Dab glue on the second section on the scallops between those glued on the first section. Press the first section on top. Continue gluing the sections at alternate positions.*

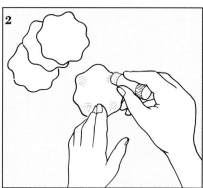

3 *Pierce a hole through the centre of the tissue sections. Insert a length of wire through the holes, dab glue on one end and push into the head. Cover 2 small cotton pulp balls with tissue, twist the ends and dab the twist with glue to secure. Cut off the twisted ends. Push the extending end of the wire into one ball.*

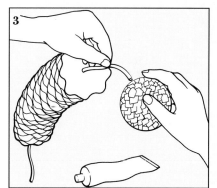

4 *Glue the first and last sections to the head and ball respectively close to the wire. Glue the remaining ball to the head as a nose. To make the antennae, bend the ends of 2 lengths of wire into hooks. Cut narrow strips of crepe paper and spread with glue. Bind around the wires. Pierce holes in the head and insert the antennae ends. Glue on joggle eyes and a coloured paper smile.*

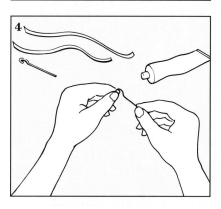

99

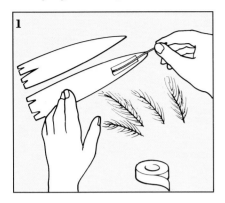

1 Use the templates on pages 121 and 122 to cut 1 upper tail, 1 lower tail, 2 top wings, 2 middle wings and 2 lower wings from black paper. Also, cut 24 black tissue paper backs and fronts, 24 white tissue paper chests and 24 blue tissue paper heads (templates on pages 121 and 122-123). Cut 2 card backs from black card along the broken lines. Using double-sided adhesive tape, attach wire along the centre line of the upper tail, extending at the straight end.

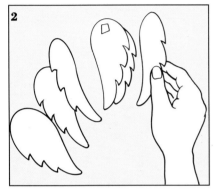

2 Stick tails together, fold in half lengthways and glue red and blue feathers underneath. Overlap heads and fronts over chests by 4 mm (⁵⁄₃₂ in) and attach with paper glue. Place the front layers on the back layers. Make up following the tissue honeycomb instructions, steps 2-4, on pages 26-27, sticking card pieces on the back and gluing the tail wire to one card back. Attach wing pieces together using double-sided adhesive tape at the top of each piece.

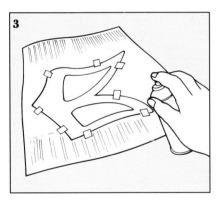

3 Glue wings to the toucan's sides. Cut upper and lower beaks (template on pages 122-123) from yellow card and cartridge paper. To make stencils, cut out areas marked on templates on the cartridge paper beaks. Attach the stencils to the yellow beaks with masking tape and spray with red spray paint. Remove stencils when the paint has dried. Cover beak points with paper. Spray the upper beak with green spray paint and the lower beak with green and blue spray paints.

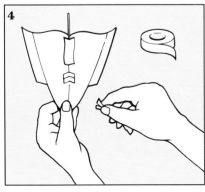

4 Score backs of beaks along broken lines. Fold forward along scored lines. Tape wire along the centre line, extending 1.5 cm (⁵⁄₈ in) at the unpointed ends. Join upper and lower edges together edge to edge with pieces of masking tape on the reverse. Stick the lower beak inside the upper beak using double-sided adhesive tape on the tabs, matching tabs to tab lines. Gloss varnish the beak.

▲ This cheerful toucan can be placed on a shelf with its claws hooked around the shelf edge for support.

▶ The use of real feathers and glass eyes make this otherwise paper penguin highly life-like and appealing.

5 *Dab glue on the beak wires and insert between head and chest sections. Glue 2-cm (¾-in) blue toy safety eyes to the head. Cut 6 pipecleaners 10 cm (4 in) long, twist 3 together for a length of 4.5 cm (1¾ in). Splay ends open to form claws. Cut narrow strips of grey paper, spread with glue and bind around the feet. Glue the ends inside the front sections.*

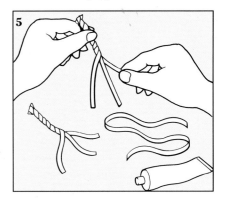

1 *To make the penguin, use templates on page 123 to cut 3 tails and 2 wings from black paper. Cut 24 black tissue paper backs and heads and 24 white tissue paper fronts (templates on pages 121 and 122). Cut 2 backs from black card along broken lines. Overlap tails at the top and glue together. Tape wire along the centre, extending at the top. Overlap heads over fronts by 4 mm (⁵/₃₂ in) and attach with paper glue. Place the front layers on the back layers.*

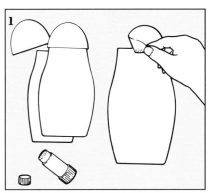

2 *Make the penguin body following the tissue honeycomb instructions, steps 2-4, on pages 26-27, attaching card pieces to the back and sticking the tail wire to one card back. Glue wings to either side of the penguin. Cut 2 feet, 1 upper beak and 1 lower beak from yellow card using the templates on pages 122-123. Score the backs along broken lines and fold forwards along scored lines. Pierce a hole in each foot at dots and insert a short pipecleaner through each hole. Glue pipecleaner ends underneath the feet.*

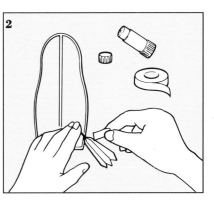

3 *Glue other ends inside the front sections. Join the upper and lower beak edges together with pieces of masking tape on the reverse. Tape wire along the joins, extending 2 cm (¾ in) at the ends. Stick the lower beak inside the upper beak using double-sided adhesive tape on the tabs, matching tabs to tab lines. Dab glue on the wires and insert inside head and front sections. Glue safety eyes to head. Glue yellow feathers above eyes.*

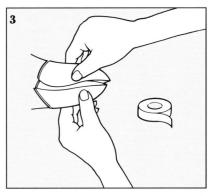

Diagrams and Templates

The following pages present the diagrams and templates for the projects. The diagrams are constructed from measurements. Use a ruler and set square to draw the pieces onto card to use as a template. It is important to follow either the metric or imperial measurements but not a combination of both.

The templates printed in blue are reduced in size. To enlarge, draw a grid of 1.4 cm (⁹⁄₁₆ in) squares. Copy the design square by square using the lines as a guide. Alternatively, enlarge templates on a photocopier to 141% (or A4 enlarged to A3). To make a complete pattern for symmetrical shapes, place the pattern on a piece of folded paper matching the 'place to fold' line to the folded edge. Cut out and open the pattern out flat to use.

SMOCKING
Page 63

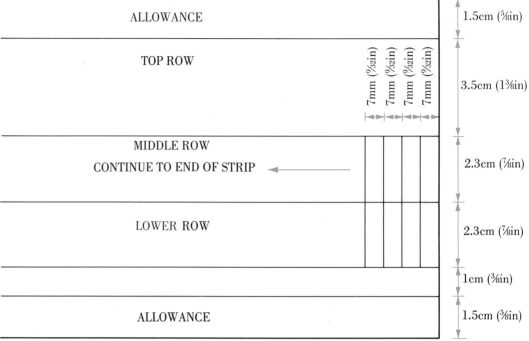

TRIANGULAR TREE
Page 48

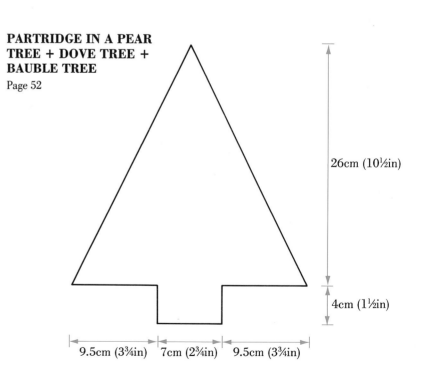

PARTRIDGE IN A PEAR TREE + DOVE TREE + BAUBLE TREE
Page 52

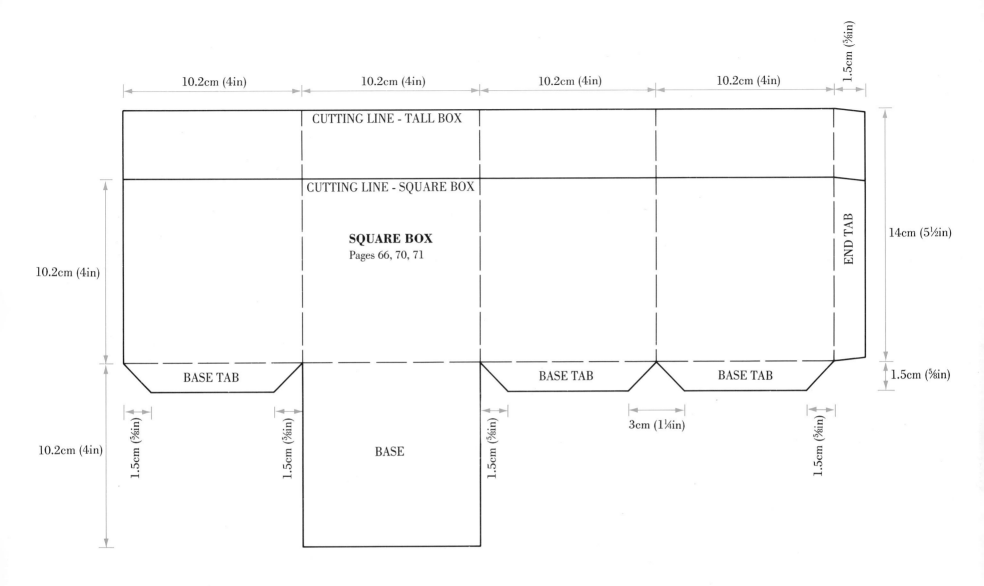

10.2cm (4in) 10.2cm (4in) 10.2cm (4in) 10.2cm (4in) 1.5cm (⅝in)

CUTTING LINE - TALL BOX

CUTTING LINE - SQUARE BOX

SQUARE BOX
Pages 66, 70, 71

END TAB

14cm (5½in)

10.2cm (4in)

1.5cm (⅝in)

BASE TAB   BASE TAB   BASE TAB

10.2cm (4in)

1.5cm (⅝in)   1.5cm (⅝in)   BASE   1.5cm (⅝in)   3cm (1¼in)   1.5cm (⅝in)

CAROUSEL RIM
Page 69

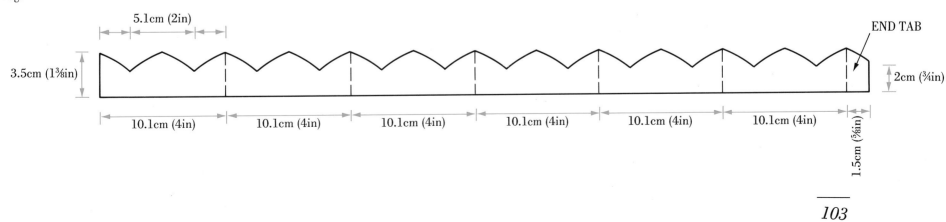

5.1cm (2in)

END TAB

3.5cm (1⅜in)

2cm (¾in)

10.1cm (4in) 10.1cm (4in) 10.1cm (4in) 10.1cm (4in) 10.1cm (4in) 10.1cm (4in) 1.5cm (⅝in)

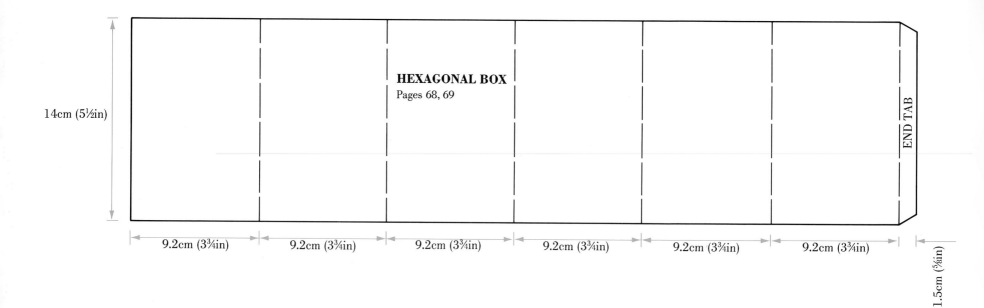

HEXAGONAL BOX
Pages 68, 69

END TAB

14cm (5½in)

9.2cm (3¾in)   9.2cm (3¾in)   9.2cm (3¾in)   9.2cm (3¾in)   9.2cm (3¾in)   9.2cm (3¾in)

1.5cm (⅝in)

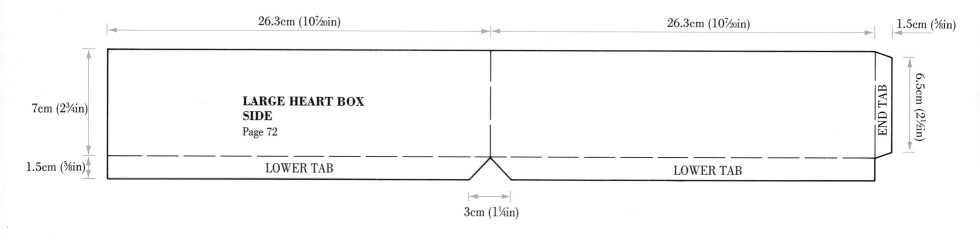

26.3cm (10⁷⁄₂₀in)   26.3cm (10⁷⁄₂₀in)   1.5cm (⅝in)

**LARGE HEART BOX
SIDE**
Page 72

END TAB

7cm (2¾in)

6.5cm (2½in)

1.5cm (⅝in)

LOWER TAB   LOWER TAB

3cm (1¼in)

LARGE HEART RIM
Page 72

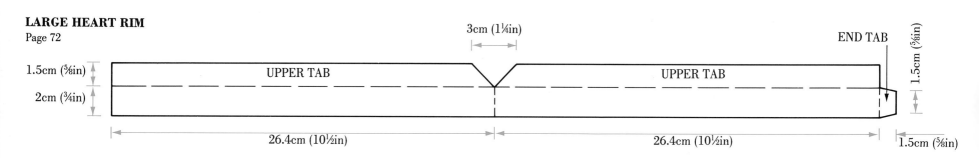

3cm (1¼in)

END TAB

1.5cm (⅝in)   UPPER TAB   UPPER TAB   1.5cm (⅝in)

2cm (¾in)

26.4cm (10½in)   26.4cm (10½in)   1.5cm (⅝in)

SQUARE POINTED LID RIM
Pages 70, 71

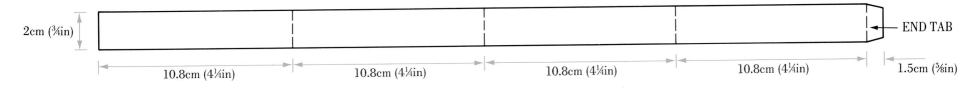

2cm (¾in)

10.8cm (4¼in) 10.8cm (4¼in) 10.8cm (4¼in) 10.8cm (4¼in)

END TAB

1.5cm (⅝in)

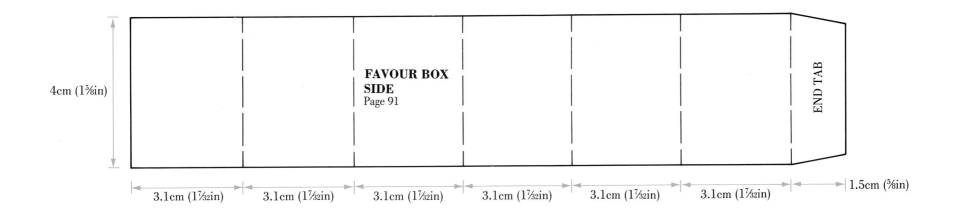

4cm (1⅝in)

FAVOUR BOX SIDE
Page 91

END TAB

3.1cm (1⅞₂in) 3.1cm (1⅞₂in) 3.1cm (1⅞₂in) 3.1cm (1⅞₂in) 3.1cm (1⅞₂in) 3.1cm (1⅞₂in)

1.5cm (⅝in)

SMALL HEART RIM
Page 73

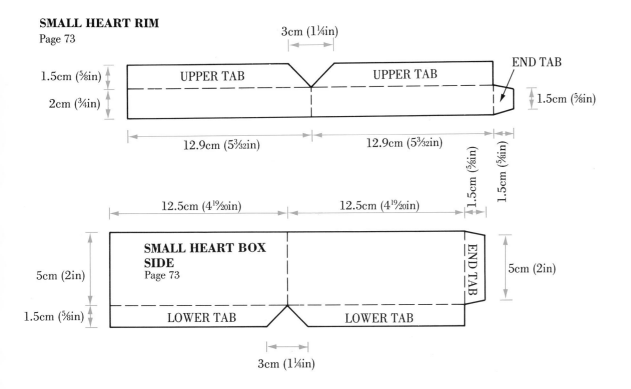

3cm (1¼in)

1.5cm (⅝in)

2cm (¾in)

UPPER TAB   UPPER TAB

END TAB

1.5cm (⅝in)

12.9cm (5³⁄₃₂in)   12.9cm (5³⁄₃₂in)

1.5cm (⅝in)   1.5cm (⅝in)

12.5cm (4¹⁹⁄₂₀in)   12.5cm (4¹⁹⁄₂₀in)

SMALL HEART BOX SIDE
Page 73

END TAB

5cm (2in)

5cm (2in)

1.5cm (⅝in)

LOWER TAB   LOWER TAB

3cm (1¼in)

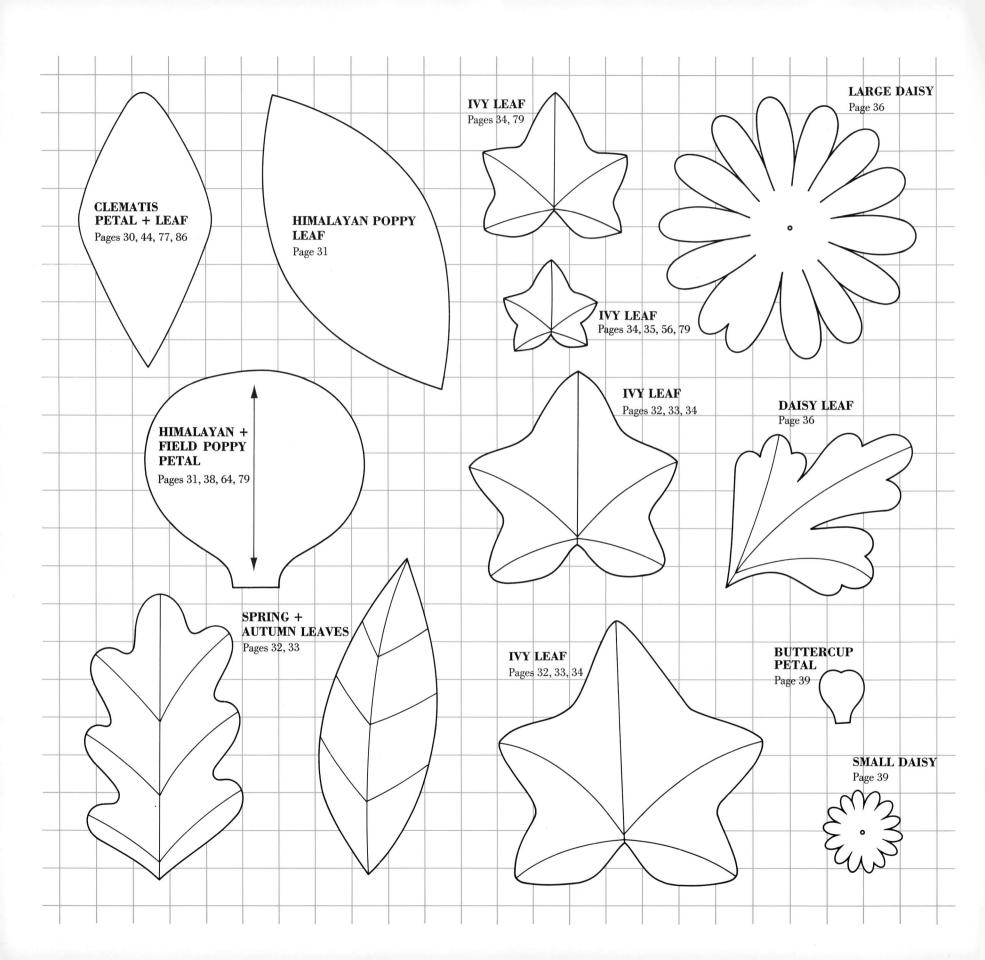

CLEMATIS PETAL + LEAF
Pages 30, 44, 77, 86

HIMALAYAN POPPY LEAF
Page 31

IVY LEAF
Pages 34, 79

LARGE DAISY
Page 36

IVY LEAF
Pages 34, 35, 56, 79

HIMALAYAN + FIELD POPPY PETAL
Pages 31, 38, 64, 79

IVY LEAF
Pages 32, 33, 34

DAISY LEAF
Page 36

SPRING + AUTUMN LEAVES
Pages 32, 33

IVY LEAF
Pages 32, 33, 34

BUTTERCUP PETAL
Page 39

SMALL DAISY
Page 39

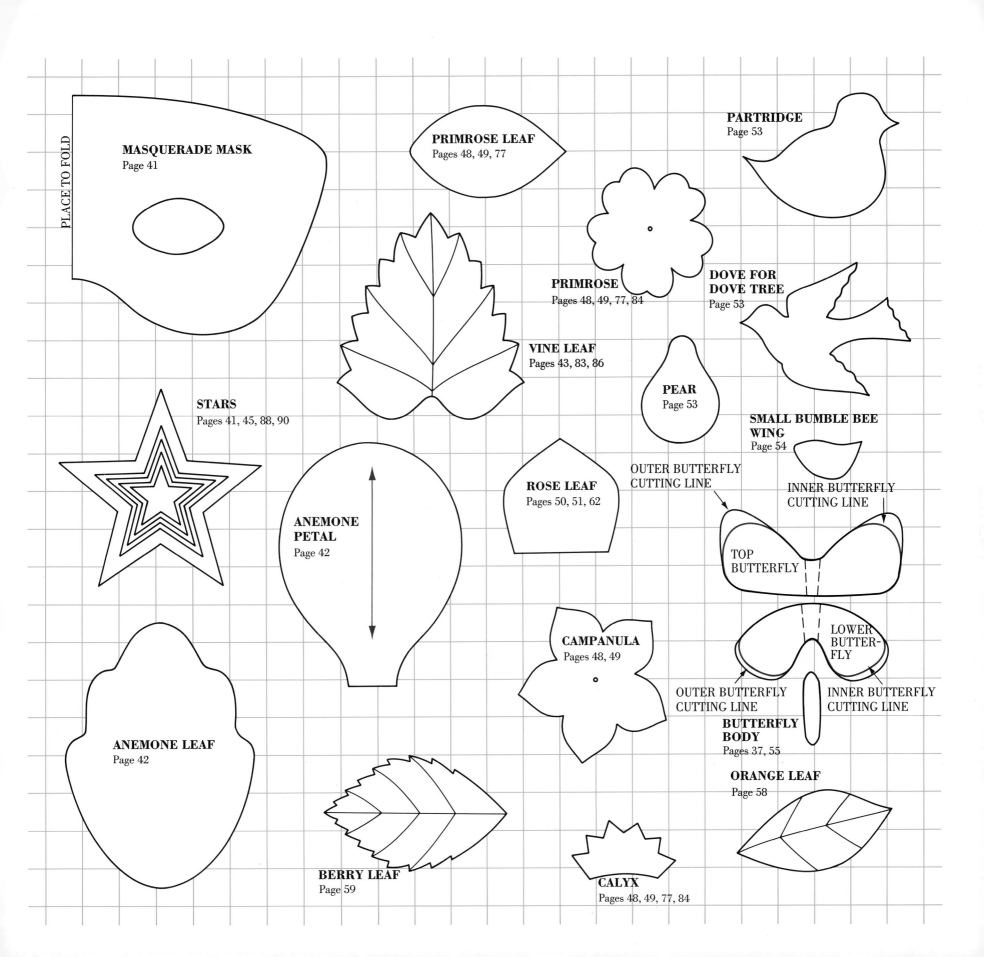

PLACE TO FOLD

MASQUERADE MASK
Page 41

PRIMROSE LEAF
Pages 48, 49, 77

PARTRIDGE
Page 53

PRIMROSE
Pages 48, 49, 77, 84

DOVE FOR DOVE TREE
Page 53

VINE LEAF
Pages 43, 83, 86

PEAR
Page 53

SMALL BUMBLE BEE WING
Page 54

STARS
Pages 41, 45, 88, 90

ROSE LEAF
Pages 50, 51, 62

OUTER BUTTERFLY CUTTING LINE

INNER BUTTERFLY CUTTING LINE

ANEMONE PETAL
Page 42

TOP BUTTERFLY

LOWER BUTTER-FLY

CAMPANULA
Pages 48, 49

OUTER BUTTERFLY CUTTING LINE

INNER BUTTERFLY CUTTING LINE

BUTTERFLY BODY
Pages 37, 55

ORANGE LEAF
Page 58

ANEMONE LEAF
Page 42

BERRY LEAF
Page 59

CALYX
Pages 48, 49, 77, 84

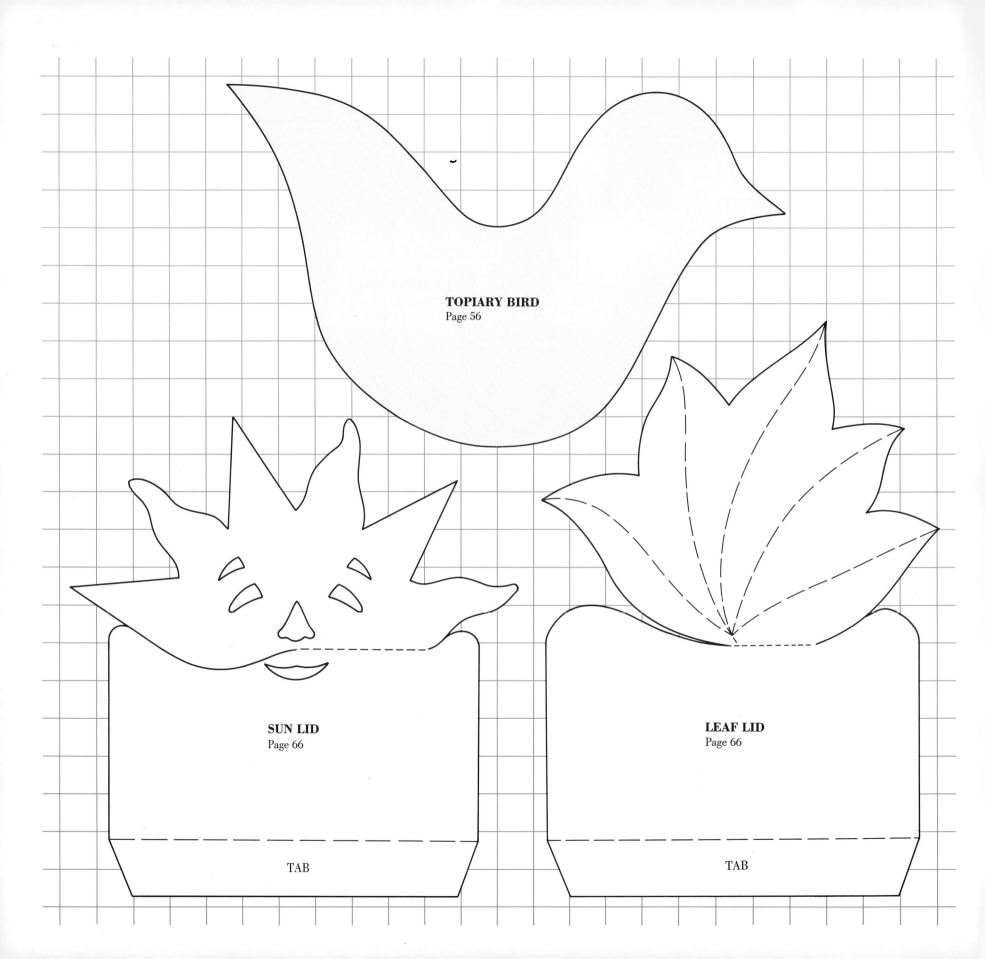

TOPIARY BIRD
Page 56

SUN LID
Page 66

LEAF LID
Page 66

TAB

TAB

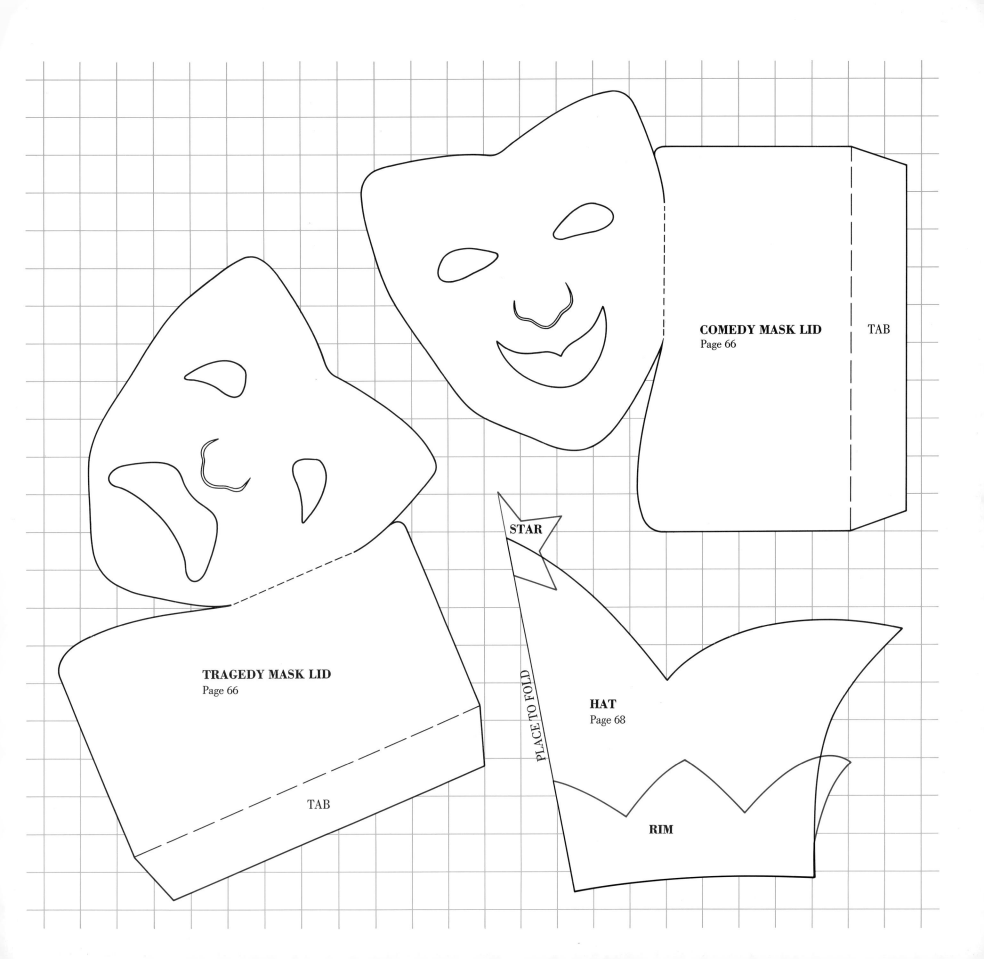

COMEDY MASK LID
Page 66

TAB

STAR

TRAGEDY MASK LID
Page 66

TAB

PLACE TO FOLD

HAT
Page 68

RIM

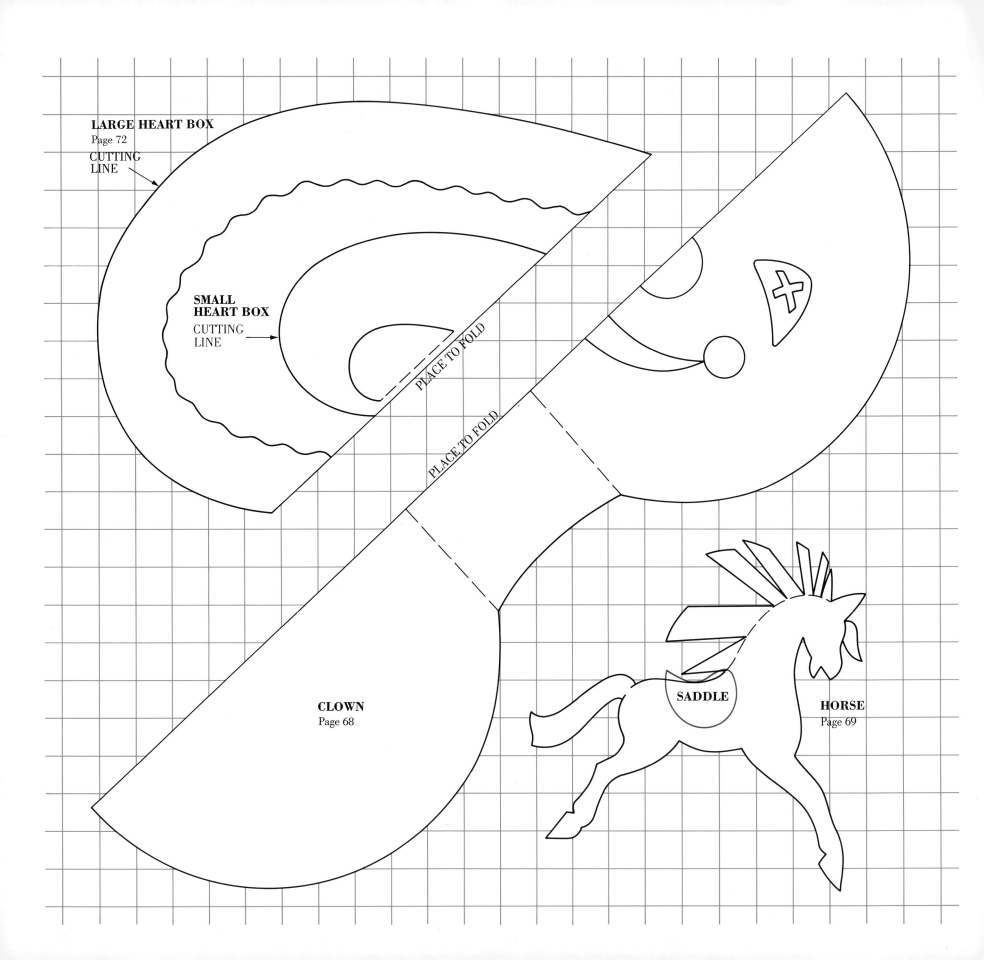

LARGE HEART BOX
Page 72
CUTTING
LINE

**SMALL
HEART BOX**
CUTTING
LINE

PLACE TO FOLD

PLACE TO FOLD

CLOWN
Page 68

SADDLE

HORSE
Page 69

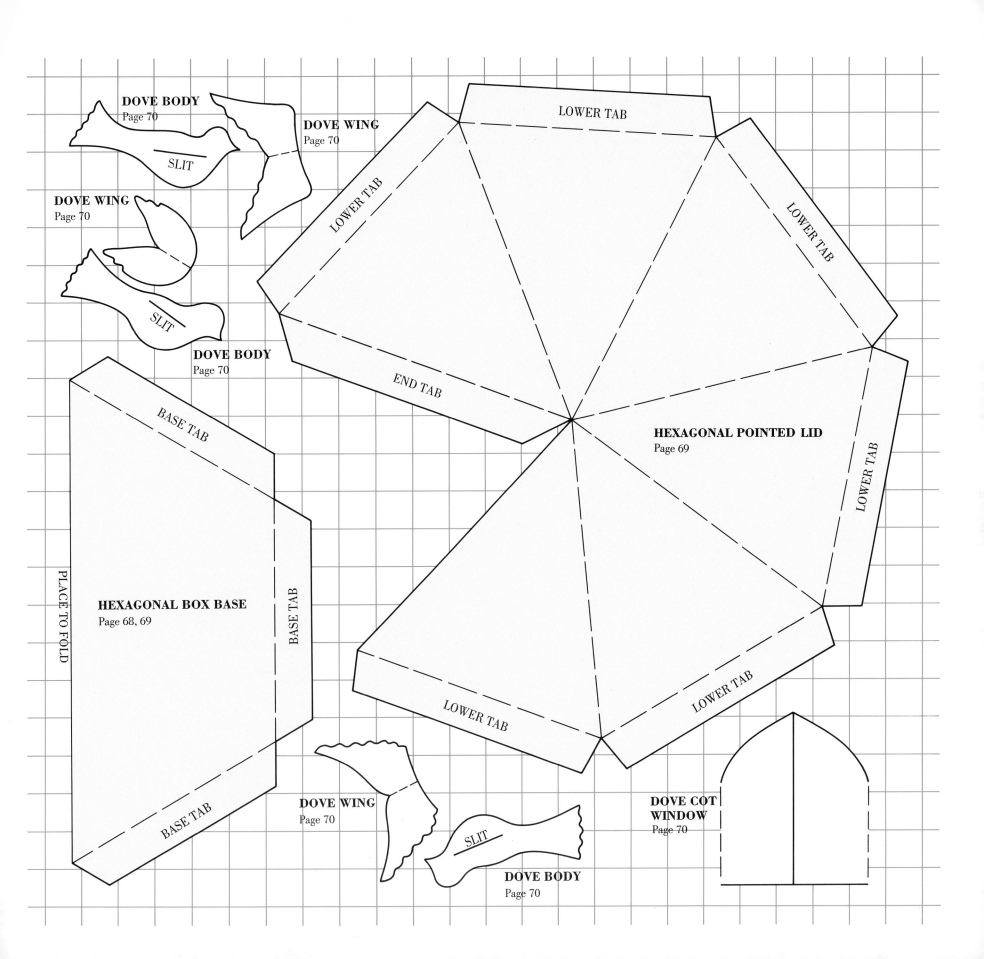

DOVE BODY
Page 70

SLIT

DOVE WING
Page 70

DOVE WING
Page 70

SLIT

DOVE BODY
Page 70

LOWER TAB

LOWER TAB

LOWER TAB

LOWER TAB

END TAB

HEXAGONAL POINTED LID
Page 69

LOWER TAB

BASE TAB

BASE TAB

PLACE TO FOLD

HEXAGONAL BOX BASE
Page 68, 69

BASE TAB

LOWER TAB

LOWER TAB

DOVE WING
Page 70

SLIT

DOVE BODY
Page 70

DOVE COT WINDOW
Page 70

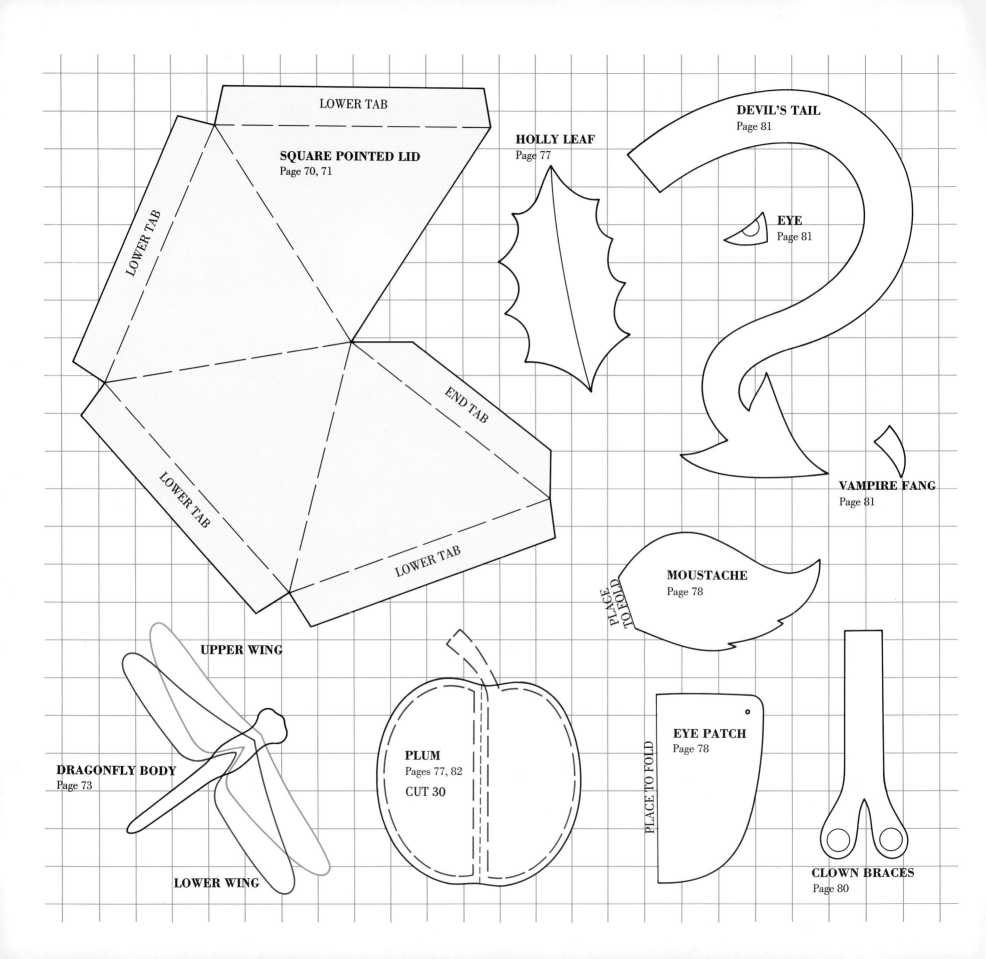

LOWER TAB

DEVIL'S TAIL
Page 81

SQUARE POINTED LID
Page 70, 71

HOLLY LEAF
Page 77

LOWER TAB

EYE
Page 81

LOWER TAB

END TAB

LOWER TAB

VAMPIRE FANG
Page 81

LOWER TAB

PLACE TO FOLD

MOUSTACHE
Page 78

UPPER WING

DRAGONFLY BODY
Page 73

PLUM
Pages 77, 82

CUT 30

PLACE TO FOLD

EYE PATCH
Page 78

LOWER WING

CLOWN BRACES
Page 80

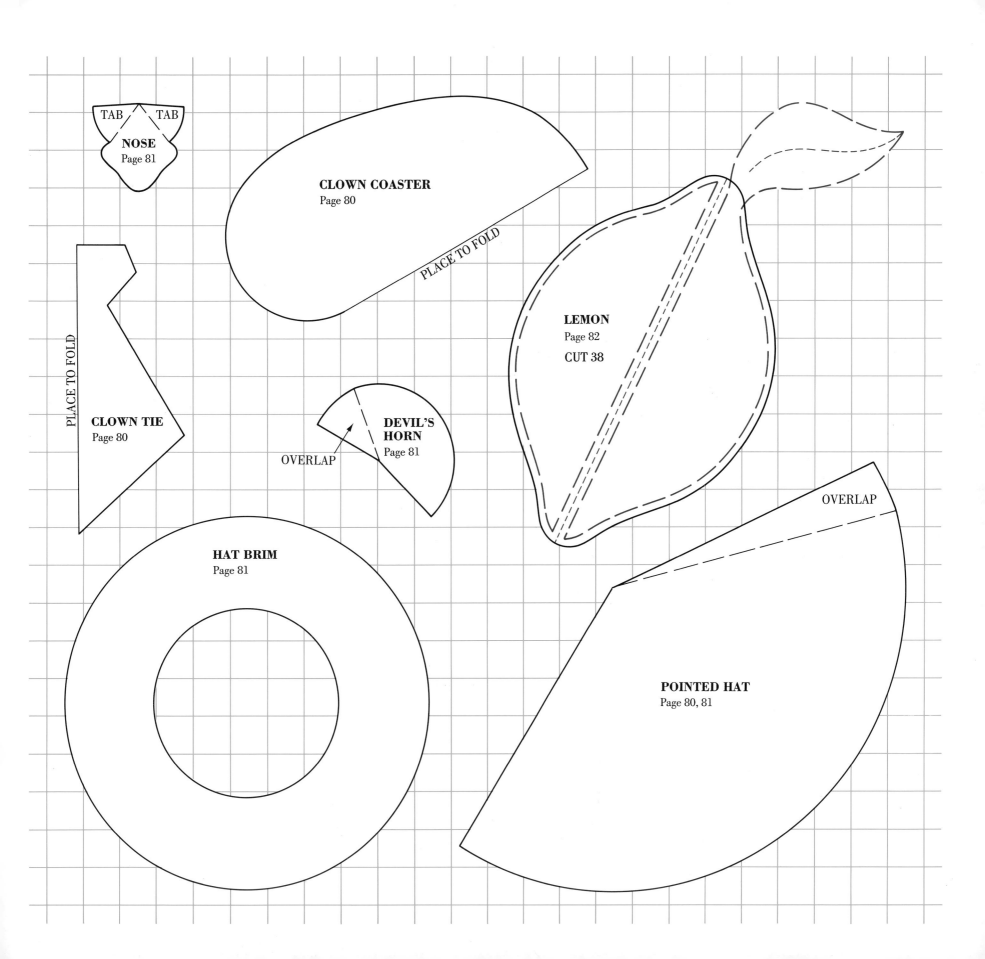

TAB TAB

NOSE
Page 81

CLOWN COASTER
Page 80

PLACE TO FOLD

LEMON
Page 82

CUT 38

PLACE TO FOLD

CLOWN TIE
Page 80

OVERLAP

DEVIL'S HORN
Page 81

OVERLAP

HAT BRIM
Page 81

POINTED HAT
Page 80, 81

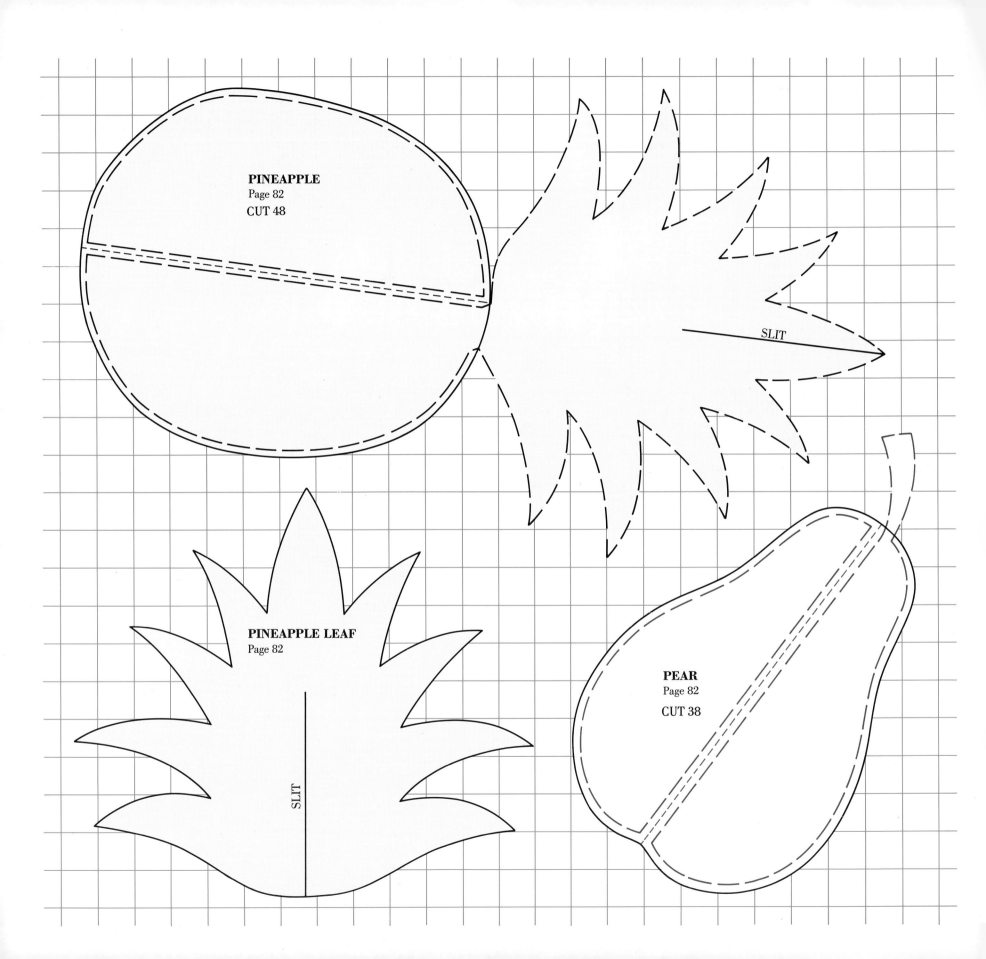

PINEAPPLE
Page 82
CUT 48

SLIT

PINEAPPLE LEAF
Page 82

SLIT

PEAR
Page 82

CUT 38

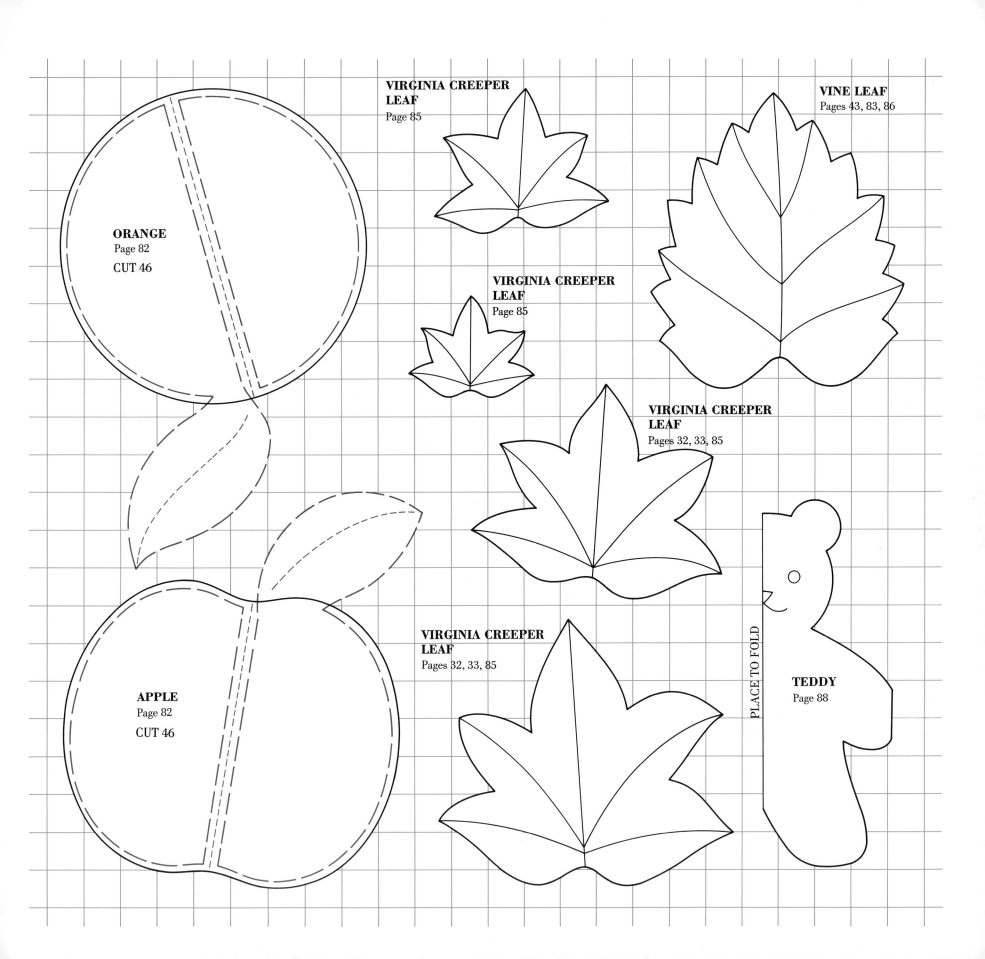

VIRGINIA CREEPER LEAF
Page 85

VINE LEAF
Pages 43, 83, 86

ORANGE
Page 82
CUT 46

VIRGINIA CREEPER LEAF
Page 85

VIRGINIA CREEPER LEAF
Pages 32, 33, 85

APPLE
Page 82
CUT 46

VIRGINIA CREEPER LEAF
Pages 32, 33, 85

PLACE TO FOLD

TEDDY
Page 88

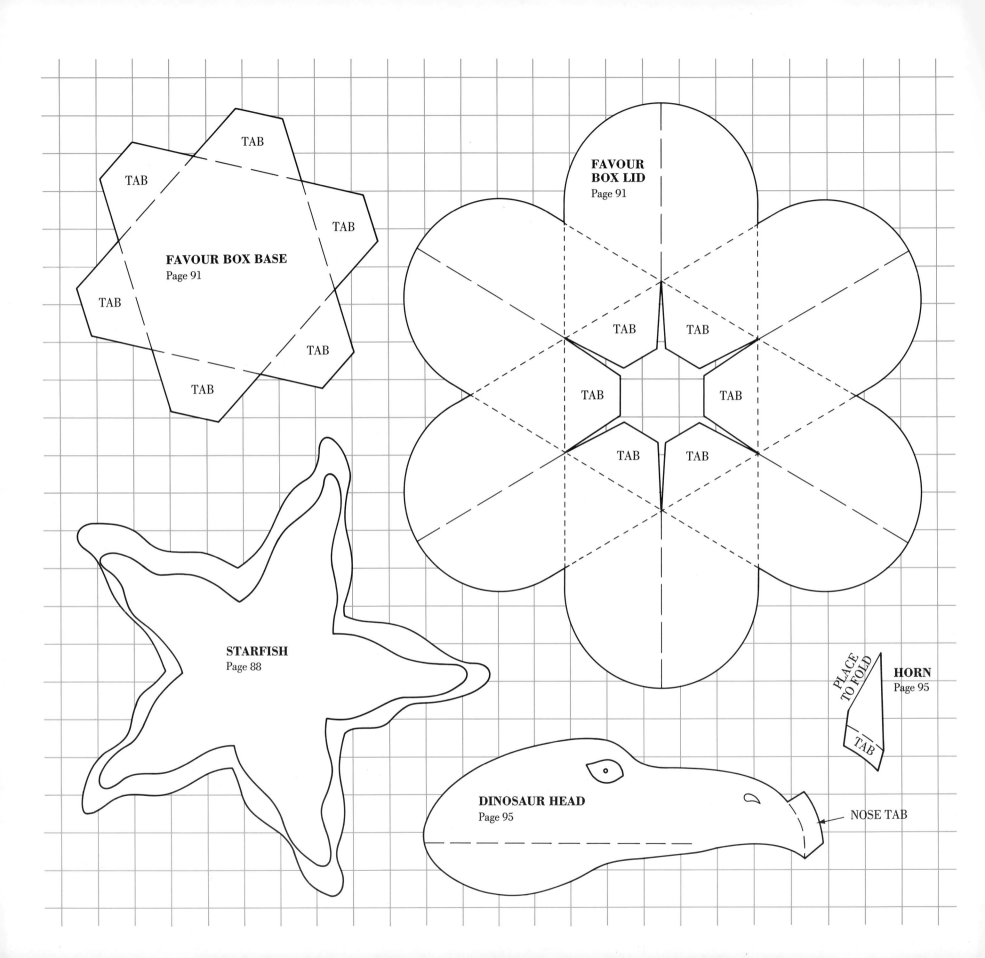

FAVOUR BOX BASE
Page 91

TAB
TAB
TAB
TAB
TAB
TAB

FAVOUR BOX LID
Page 91

TAB
TAB
TAB
TAB
TAB
TAB

STARFISH
Page 88

HORN
Page 95

PLACE TO FOLD

TAB

DINOSAUR HEAD
Page 95

NOSE TAB

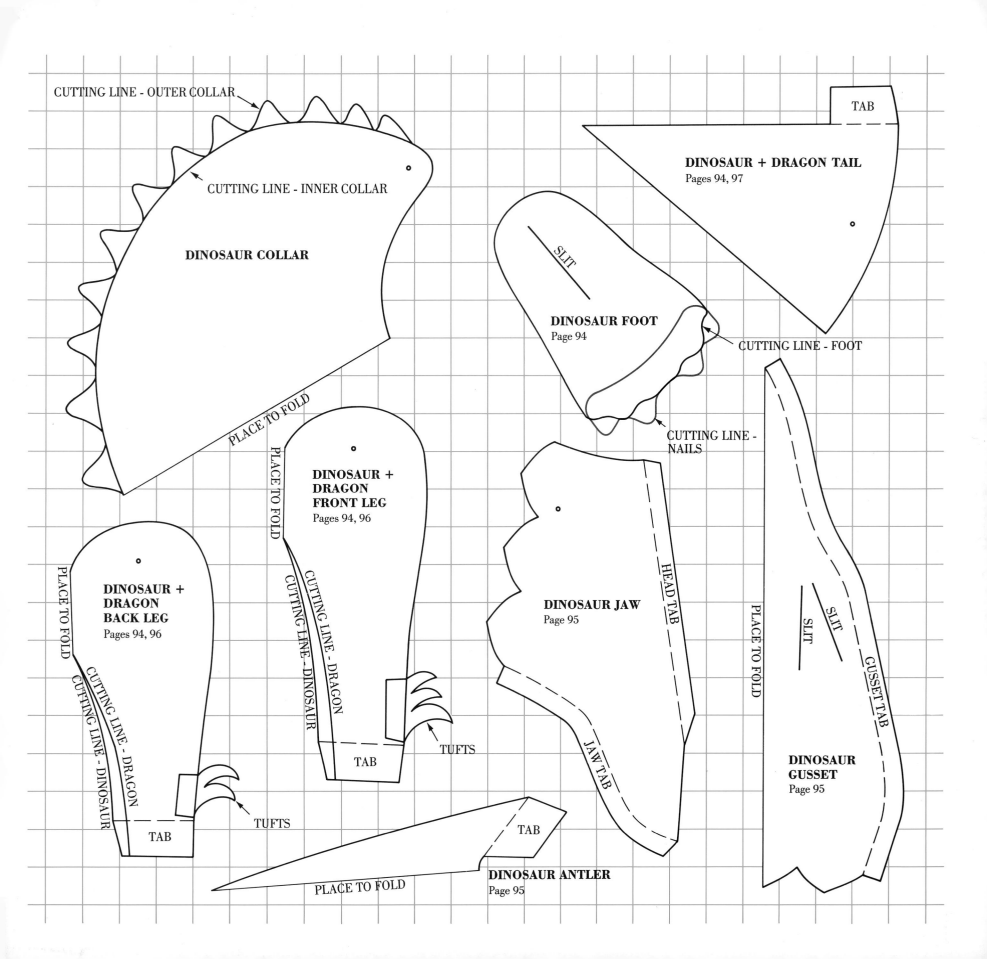

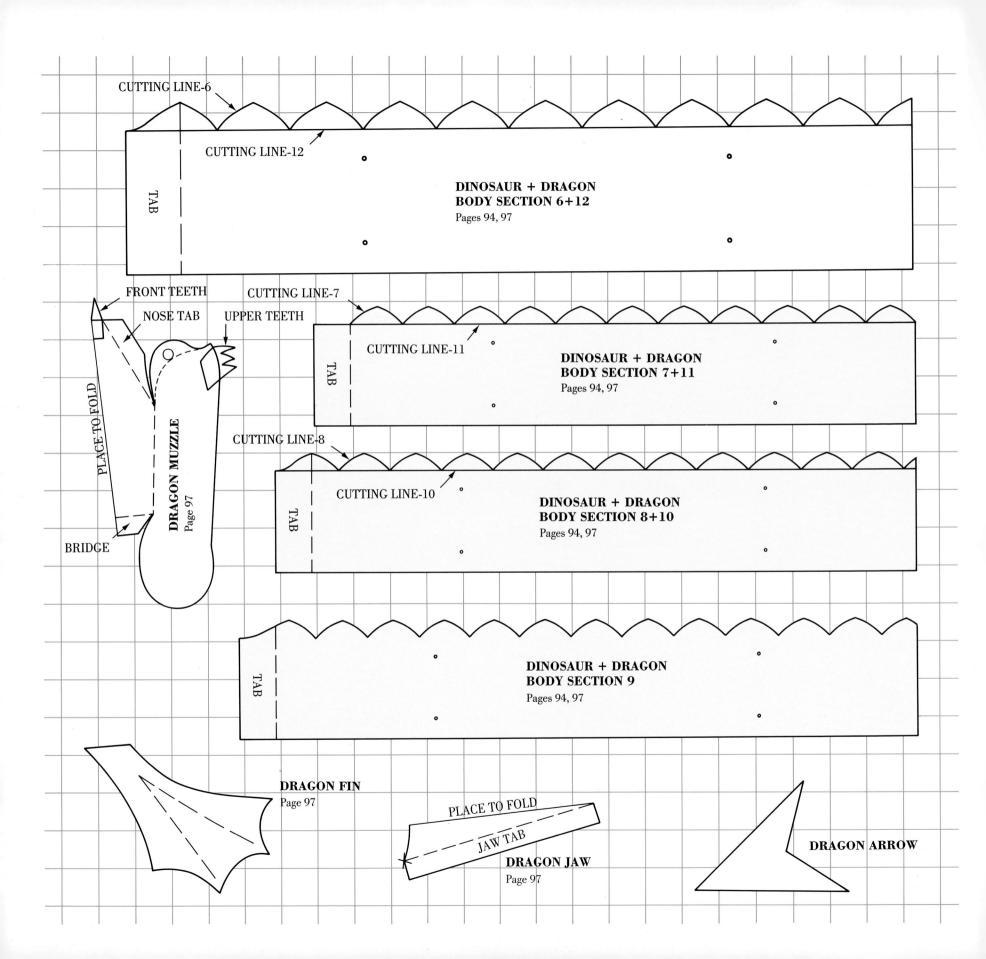

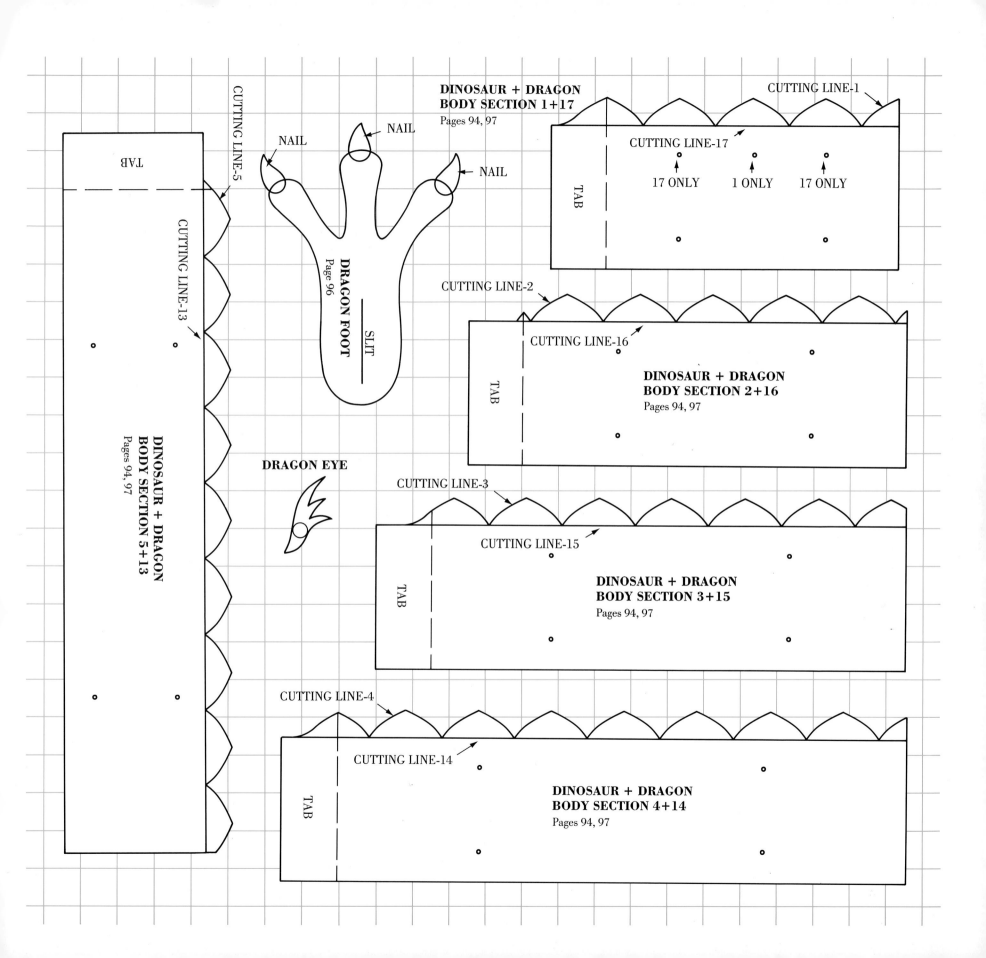

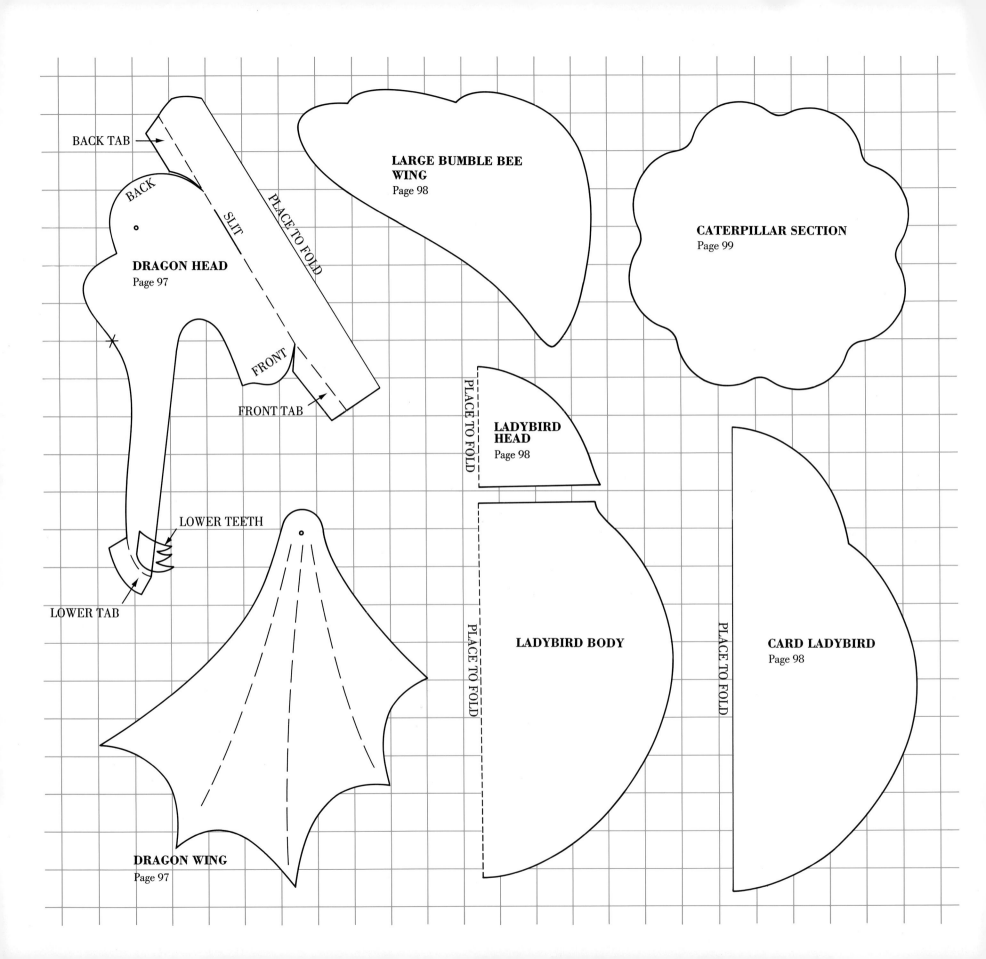

BACK TAB

BACK

SLIT

PLACE TO FOLD

DRAGON HEAD
Page 97

FRONT

FRONT TAB

LARGE BUMBLE BEE WING
Page 98

CATERPILLAR SECTION
Page 99

PLACE TO FOLD

LADYBIRD HEAD
Page 98

LOWER TEETH

LOWER TAB

PLACE TO FOLD

LADYBIRD BODY

PLACE TO FOLD

CARD LADYBIRD
Page 98

DRAGON WING
Page 97

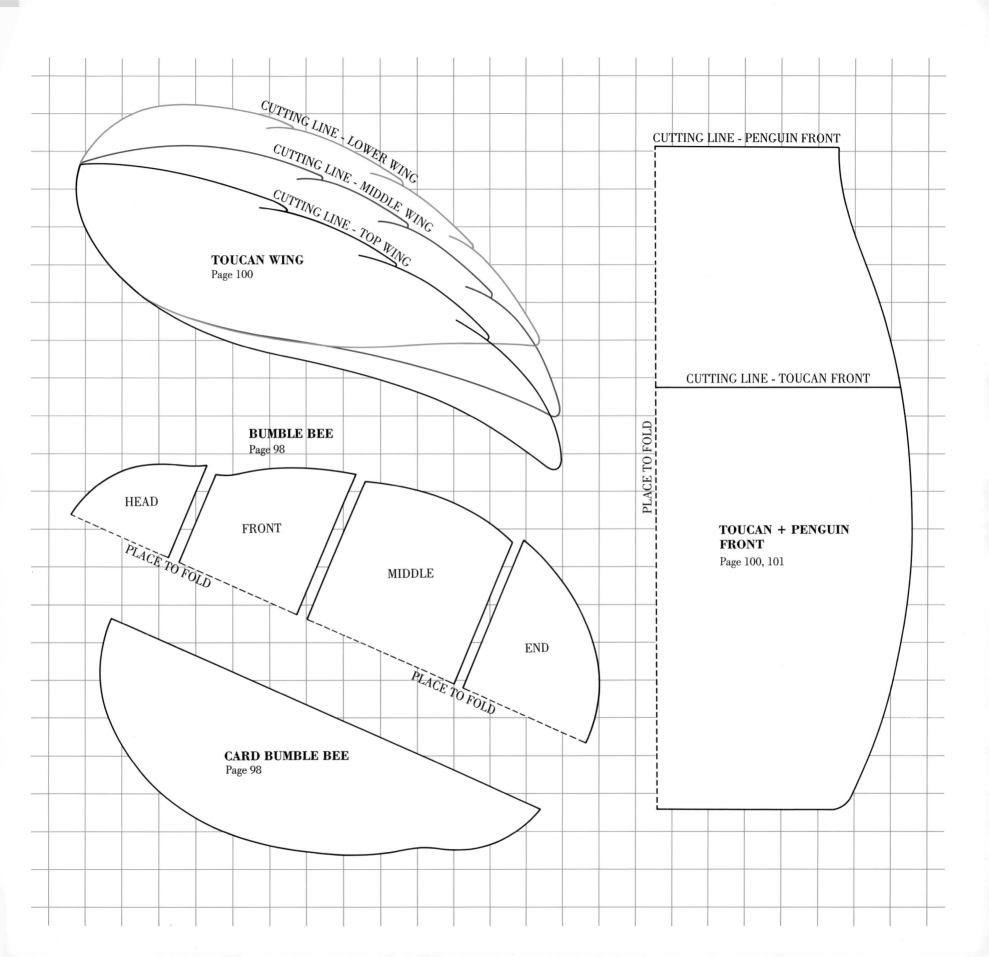

CUTTING LINE - LOWER WING

CUTTING LINE - MIDDLE WING

CUTTING LINE - TOP WING

TOUCAN WING
Page 100

CUTTING LINE - PENGUIN FRONT

CUTTING LINE - TOUCAN FRONT

PLACE TO FOLD

TOUCAN + PENGUIN FRONT
Page 100, 101

BUMBLE BEE
Page 98

HEAD

FRONT

MIDDLE

END

PLACE TO FOLD

PLACE TO FOLD

CARD BUMBLE BEE
Page 98

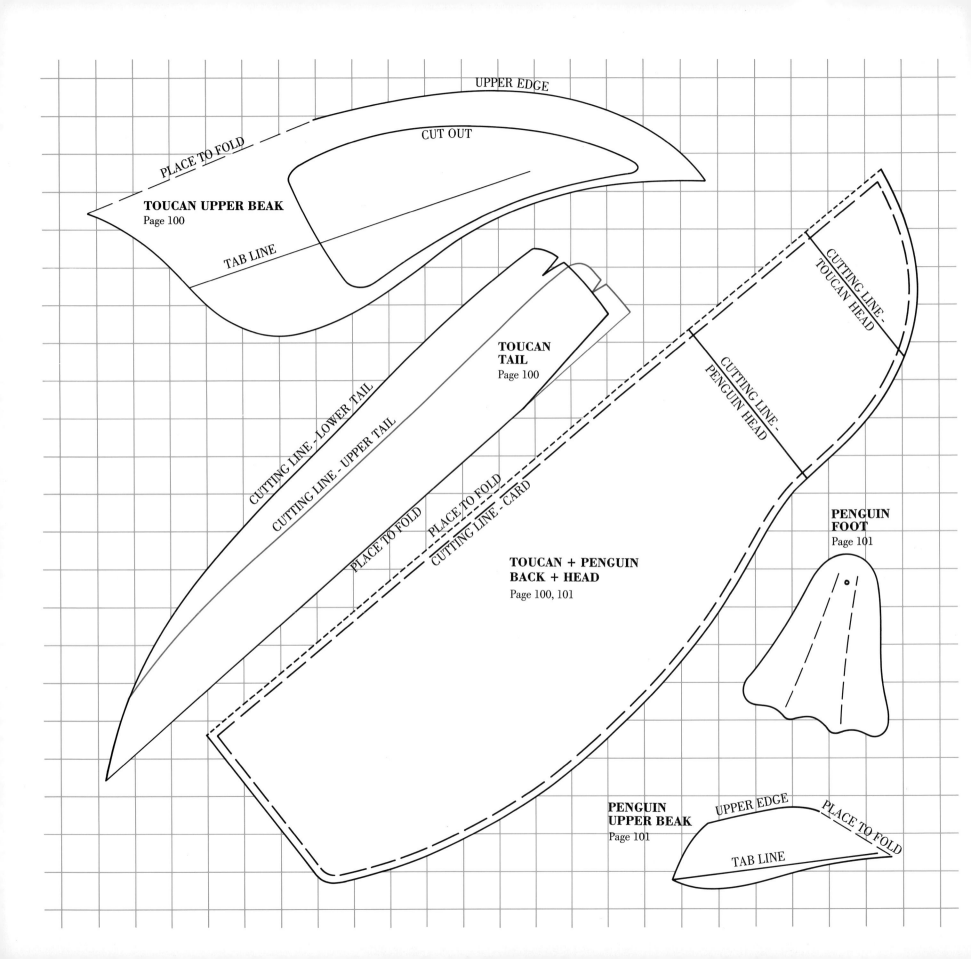

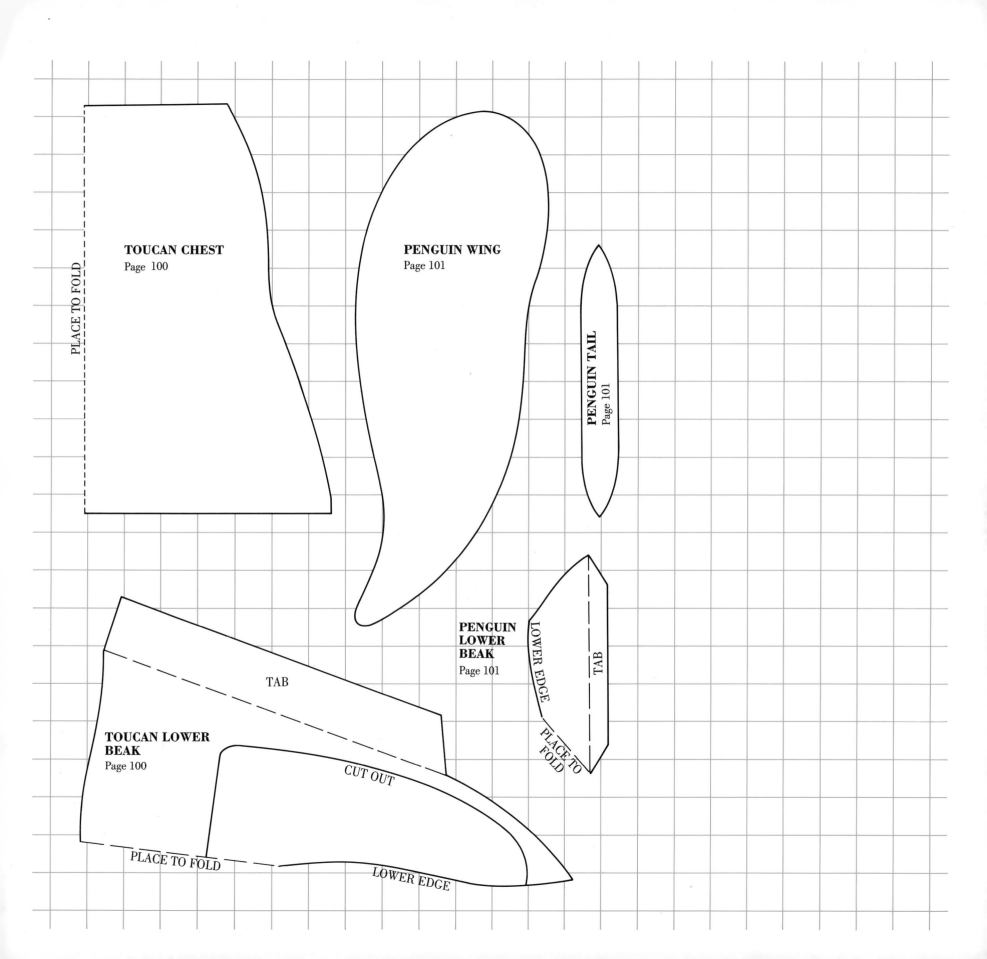

TOUCAN CHEST
Page 100

PLACE TO FOLD

PENGUIN WING
Page 101

PENGUIN TAIL
Page 101

PENGUIN LOWER BEAK
Page 101

LOWER EDGE

PLACE TO FOLD

TAB

TAB

TOUCAN LOWER BEAK
Page 100

CUT OUT

PLACE TO FOLD

LOWER EDGE

AUTHOR'S ACKNOWLEDGEMENT

The author would like to thank The Handicraft Shop, Northgate, Canterbury CT1 1BE (Tel: 0227 451188) for supplying various craft materials used in the projects.

Editorial: Jo Finnis

Design: Alison Jewell

Photography: Neil Sutherland; Steve Tanner; Peter Barry

Photographic Direction: Roger Hyde; Nigel Duffield

Illustration: Geoff Denney Associates; Richard Hawke
(diagrams and templates)

Typesetting: Julie Smith

Production: Ruth Arthur; Sally Connolly;
Andrew Whitelaw; Neil Randles

Director of Production: Gerald Hughes